CORE SKILLS

GRADE **3**

Test Preparation

Strategies for
- *Reading*
- *Vocabulary*
- *Math*
- *Listening*
- *Language*

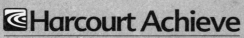

Harcourt Achieve

Rigby • Saxon • Steck-Vaughn

www.HarcourtAchieve.com
1.800.531.5015

Core Skills: Test Preparation
Grade 3
Contents

ISBN 0-7398-5736-3

6 7 8 9 054 09 08 07 06 05

Dear Parent,

Welcome to *Steck-Vaughn Core Skills: Test Preparation*. You have selected a book that will help your child develop the skills he or she needs to succeed on standardized tests.

Although testing can be a source of anxiety for children, this book will give your child the preparation and practice that he or she needs to feel better prepared and more confident when taking a standardized test. Research shows that children who are acquainted with the scoring format of standardized tests score higher on those tests. Students also score higher when they practice and understand the skills and strategies needed to take standardized tests. The subject areas and concepts presented in this book are typically found on standardized tests at this grade level.

To best help your child, please consider the following suggestions:

- Provide a quiet place to work.
- Go over the directions and the sample exercises together.
- Review the strategy tips.
- Reassure your child that the practice tests are not "real" tests.
- Encourage your child to do his or her best.
- Check the lesson when it is complete.
- Go over the answers and note improvements as well as problems.

If your child expresses anxiety about taking a test or completing these lessons, help him or her understand what causes the stress. Then, talk about ways to eliminate anxiety. Above all, enjoy this time you spend with your child. He or she will feel your support, and test scores will improve as success in test taking is experienced.

Help your child maintain a positive attitude about taking a standardized test. Let your child know that each test provides an opportunity to shine.

Sincerely,

The Educators and Staff of
Steck-Vaughn School Supply

P.S. You might want to visit our website at **www.svschoolsupply.com** for more test preparation materials as well as additional review of content areas.

Dear Student,

Sometime during the school year, you will be taking standardized tests. This book can help you prepare to take such tests.

Here are some suggestions for using these practice tests and for taking the "real" tests.

DO:
- Listen to or read all the directions.
- Read the **Try This** strategy tips, do the **Sample** items, and then look at **Think It Through** to check your answer before you begin each lesson.
- Look over the entire test or section before you begin.
- Stay calm, concentrate on the test, and clear your mind of things that have nothing to do with the test.
- Read all the answer choices before choosing the one that you think is best.
- Make sure the number you fill in on the answer sheet matches the question number on the test page.
- Trust your first instinct when answering each question.
- Answer the easy questions first, then go back and work on the ones you aren't sure about.
- Take all the time you are allowed.

DON'T:
- Look ahead to another question until you complete the one you're working on.
- Spend too much time on one question.
- Rush.
- Worry if others finish while you are still working.
- Change an answer unless you are really sure it should be changed.

Remember to do your best!

Core Skills: Test Preparation

Introduction

Standardized tests are becoming increasingly more important in both public and private schools, yet test anxiety causes many children to perform below their fullest potential. *Core Skills: Test Preparation* is designed to help children succeed on standardized tests. This program refreshes basic skills, familiarizes children with test formats and directions, and teaches test-taking strategies.

A large part of being well prepared for a test is knowing how to approach different types of questions and learning how to use time wisely. *Core Skills: Test Preparation* gives children the opportunity to take a test under conditions that parallel those they will face when taking standardized tests. This practice and experience will allow them to feel more confident when taking standardized tests and will enable them to demonstrate their knowledge successfully.

Tools for Success

Core Skills: Test Preparation gives children valuable practice with the content areas and question formats of the major standardized tests used nationally. These include:

- CAT (California Achievement Tests)
- CTBS (Comprehensive Tests of Basic Skills)
- FCAT (Florida Comprehensive Assessment Tests)
- ITBS (Iowa Tests of Basic Skills)
- SAT (Stanford Achievement Test)
- TAKS (Texas Assessment of Knowledge and Skills)
- TerraNova

Core Skills: Test Preparation provides:
- Test-taking strategies
- Familiarity with test directions
- Review of skills and content
- Awareness of test formats
- Practice tests

Organization

The book is divided into units that correspond to those found on standardized tests. These include:

- Reading Comprehension
- Reading Vocabulary
- Mathematics Problem Solving
- Mathematics Procedures
- Listening
- Language

Core Skills: Test Preparation is designed to ensure success on test day by offering:

Strategies for Taking Reading Tests

Unit 1 provides valuable test-taking strategies to help your child do his or her best on the reading portion of any standardized test.

Targeted Reading Objectives

Unit 2 focuses on six reading objectives. Each practice question includes a hint to help your child master the targeted objective.

Strategies for Solving Math Problems

Unit 5 offers a step-by-step approach to solving word problems.

Skill Lessons

Units 3, 4, 6, 7, and 8 prepare your child by providing both content review and test-taking strategies. Each skill lesson includes:

Directions—states test instructions clearly, concisely, and in a format similar to that of standardized tests
Try This—offers a test strategy that helps children approach each question in a logical way
A *Sample*—familiarizes children with the "look and feel" of test items
Think It Through—specifically explains the correct answer to the sample
A *Practice Section*—contains a set of practice items that are focused on a specific skill and modeled on items from standardized tests
A *Unit Test*—covers all the skills in the lesson

Practice Tests

Units 9–13 simulate the content and format your child will encounter when taking standardized tests in reading comprehension, vocabulary, math, listening, and language.

Use

Try This and Think It Through

The *Try This* and *Think It Through* features accompany the sample questions on the skill lesson pages. Before your child answers the sample question, go over the *Try This* skill strategy by reading it aloud. Give your child time to answer the question, and then review the correct answer using the *Think It Through* feature.

Answering the Questions

Answer Bubbles—You may want to go over how to fill in the multiple choice bubble-in answers. Stress the importance of filling the answer bubble completely, pressing firmly with the pencil, and erasing any stray marks.

Short Answer Questions—Standardized tests also require children to answer questions using their own words. *Core Skills: Test Preparation* gives children practice answering this type of question.

Scripts for Listening Tests

The lessons and tests in Unit 7 (pages 78–81) and Unit 12 (pages 118–119) require that an adult read a scripted text while the child answers the questions. These scripts are collected in the section titled *Listening Scripts* on pages P6–P10. The pages are perforated so that you can remove them easily. This way, your child can mark the answers in the book while you read from the loose pages.

Practice Tests

The six practice tests, pages 97–128, simulate standardized tests, providing your child with valuable practice before test day. Like standardized tests, these are timed. The following are the suggested times needed to administer each test:

Reading Comprehension	30 minutes
Reading Vocabulary	15 minutes
Math Problem Solving	50 minutes
Math Procedures	25 minutes
Listening	20 minutes
Language	30 minutes

Answer Key

A complete answer key is found on pages 129–132. These pages are perforated so that you can remove them easily and return the book to your child.

Individual Record Form

The **Individual Record Form** found on page 133 can be used to track progress through the book and to record the child's scores on the lessons, unit tests, and practice tests.

Icons

This book contains the following icons to help you and your child:

 The **Go On** icon tells your child that the test continues on the next page.

 The **Stop** icon tells your child to stop working.

 The **Listen** icon tells you and your child that it is time to work together. Turn to the *Listening Scripts* section (pages P6–P10) to locate the script you need.

The stopwatch icon indicates the amount of time to allot for each **Practice Test**.

Core Skills: Test Preparation lessons and practice tests provide children with the tools they need to build self-confidence. That self-confidence can translate into a positive test-taking experience and higher scores on standardized tests. With its emphasis on skills, strategies for success, and practice, *Core Skills: Test Preparation* gives children the ability to succeed on standardized tests.

Standardized Test Content Areas

The following skills are tested on most standardized exams. These same skills are included in *Core Skills: Test Preparation, Grade 3*.

Reading Skills

Identifying synonyms

Using sentence context to determine word meaning of multiple-meaning words

Using sentence context to determine word meaning

Understanding explicitly stated details, actions, reasons, sequence of events

Making inferences

Inferring meaning

Extending meaning

Making predictions

Understanding implicit ideas

Identifying author's purpose

Using definitional phrases to determine word meaning

Recalling details and sequence

Drawing conclusions

Language Skills

Identifying appropriate sources of information

Using parts of a book to locate information

Determining appropriate prewriting activities

Alphabetizing words

Understanding dictionary entries

Evaluating prewriting strategies

Determining the relevance of ideas

Determining the purpose for writing

Evaluating importance of ideas

Recognizing well-constructed sentences

Recognizing correctly combined sentences

Identifying topic sentences in paragraphs

Identifying appropriate topic and concluding sentences

Recognizing sentence fragments

Identifying the correct tense of verbs

Using correct punctuation

Using correct capitalization

Understanding subject-verb agreement in number

Identifying misspelled words in sentences

Mathematics Skills

Identifying odd and even numbers

Recognizing numerals

Understanding place value

Comparing and ordering numbers

Understanding families of number facts and the properties of whole numbers

Understanding fundamental operations and fractional parts

Comparing and ordering fractions and decimals

Recognizing and interpreting number patterns and geometric patterns

Reading and interpreting bar graphs, tables, and tally charts

Determining simple probability

Recognizing geometric shapes

Understanding basic properties of plane figures and rotations

Identifying congruent figures and common solid figures

Identifying units of measurement

Measuring and comparing time and length using standard and nonstandard measurement units

Determining the value of currency

Determining solution sentences for fundamental operations

Identifying missing information

Using estimation in problem solving

Identifying reasonableness

Solving problems using logic

Adding, subtracting, multiplying, and dividing whole numbers

Rounding

Adding and subtracting whole numbers, decimals, and money in context

Multiplying whole numbers in context

Listening Scripts

These scripts accompany the listening portions of the lessons and tests found in Unit 7 on pages 78–81 and in Unit 12 on pages 118 and 119. For the lessons in Unit 7, read the directions and the **Try This** strategy to your child before doing the sample question. After completing the sample question, go over the correct answer using **Think It Through**. Then begin the lesson. In the Unit 7 and 12 tests, do the sample question at the top of the page before beginning the test. In all listening lessons and tests, give your child time to respond before reading the next question. You may read these items twice if needed.

Unit 7: Listening

Listening for Word Meanings, p. 78

Reading Skill: Using definitional phrases to determine word meaning

Look at Sample A. You will find the word that best completes the sentence. Listen carefully. I will read a sentence, followed by four answer choices. I'd like my parents to consider getting a pet. To consider something is to— A forget about it …B guess about it …C ignore it …D think about it.

Now you will practice choosing more words or groups of words that best complete sentences. We will do numbers 1 through 8. Listen carefully to the sentences and the four answer choices. Then darken the circle for the correct answer.

1   The hot air balloon began to descend slowly. Something that descends— A goes down … B drifts …C expands …D spreads out.
2   We'll take nourishing food for the camp out. Nourishing means— F tasty …G healthy … H filling …J sickening.
3   Since I studied, I'm not anxious about the test. Anxious means—A worried …B calm … C thrilled …D forgetful.
4   There was intense heat coming from the blaze. Intense means— F very little …G extreme … H moderate …J limited.
5   Marco kept his toy shelf tidy. Something that is tidy is— A small …B quick …C neat …D tired.
6   The runner moved swiftly around the track. Swiftly means— F slowly …G quickly …H quietly … J heavily.
7   I only had time to glimpse the paper. To glimpse means to— A glance …B stare …C gaze … D observe.
8   We had to pay a toll to cross the bridge. A toll is a— F fee …G allowance …H discount …J loan.

Building Listening Skills, p. 79

Reading Skill: Recalling details and sequence; drawing conclusions; making inferences; extending meaning

Look at Sample A. I will read a story and then ask a question. You will choose the best answer to the question. Listen carefully. Josh went to the store. He bought some balloons and whistles for his birthday party next week. Then he bought a kite to fly in the park with his big brother.

Now look at Sample A. Listen carefully. Josh and his brother will— A blow up balloons …B fly a kite … C blow whistles … D run a race. Darken the circle for the correct answer.

Now you will practice choosing words and phrases that best answer questions about other paragraphs and stories that you hear. We will do numbers 1 through 8. Listen to the story and the question. Then darken the circle for the correct answer.

Now find number 1. Listen as I read this story. You will answer two questions.

The caterpillar makes a cocoon from a silky thread in its body. It fastens the thread to the branch of a tree and spins a cocoon around itself. There it hangs, inside the cocoon, until it turns into a butterfly. When it is ready, it breaks open the cocoon and crawls out.

1   The caterpillar turns into a— A mosquito … B spider …C butterfly …D lady bug.
2   The caterpillar makes its cocoon from— F leaves …G silky thread …H cotton …J twigs.

Listen as I read these directions for making breakfast. You will answer two questions about the directions.

1. First, take the eggs, bread, and milk out of the refrigerator.
2. Second, put the bread in the toaster, and toast it until it is brown.
3. Next, break the eggs, and use a fork to mix them with milk.
4. Finally, scramble the eggs in a pan on the stove.
5. When your breakfast is ready, enjoy!

3 These directions tell you how to make— A fried eggs and biscuits …B cheese sandwiches … C pancakes … D scrambled eggs and toast.

4 These directions tell you to mix the eggs with— F milk … G butter …H water …J bread.

Now find number 5. Listen as I read this story. You will answer two questions.

Pam has just lost her tooth. She is happy it fell out. It had been loose for seven days. Now she can eat without feeling any pain.

5 Pam lost her tooth—A today …B seven days ago …C last month …D two weeks ago.

6 Now it will be easier for Pam to— F smile … G talk …H eat …J sleep.

Now find number 7. Listen as I read this poem.

You will answer two questions.
Ralph Rabbit said,
Oh, what a day
To eat cabbages and carrots and lettuce.
I wonder if Farmer Fred
Will chase us away or let us!

7 Ralph Rabbit did not want to eat— A carrots … B lettuce … C grass …D cabbage.

8 Fred is a— F frog …G rabbit …H little boy … J farmer.

Test, pp. 80–81

In this test you will use the listening skills we have practiced in this unit. This test is divided into two parts. For each part there is a sample exercise. Look at Sample A. In this part of the test, you will choose words or groups of words that best complete sentences. Listen carefully. I will read part of a sentence and four words. You will find the word that best completes the sentence. Aunt Sara is going to install new carpeting in her house. To install means to— A put in …B tear out …C plan …D order. Darken the circle for the correct answer.

You should have darkened the circle for A, put in, because to install is to put in.

Now you will choose more words or groups of words that best complete sentences. Find number 1. We will do numbers 1 through 12 just as we did Sample A. Listen carefully to the sentence and the four answer choices. Then darken the circle for the correct answer.

1 Let's see if we can unravel this mystery. To unravel is to— A solve …B tie again … C create … D convince.

2 The author was fascinating to hear. Fascinating means— F friendly …G interesting …H dull … J talkative.

3 I can't remember where I've heard that melody before. A melody is a— A tune …B orchestra … C noise …D singer.

4 Since we didn't have much time, it was a hasty trip. Hasty means— F careful …G hurried … H foolish …J important.

5 My father resembles my grandmother. To resemble someone means to— A talk about her …B admire her …C look like her … D try to act like her.

6 This old book is extremely rare. Rare means— F common …G beautiful …H expensive … J unusual.

7 Mom asked us not to speak very loudly in the house. To speak very loudly is to— A mumble … B laugh …C shout …D whisper.

8 The new puppy was clumsy as he tried to chase us. Clumsy means— F skillful …G smooth … H awkward … J dangerous.

9 Maya wants to invent a machine to help pick up toys. To invent is to— A make something new … B find something new …C notice something new …D misplace something new.

10 Jamal and his family adore his new baby brother. To adore means to— F take care of …G become tired of …H make fun of …J cherish.

11 Jeff visits his physician at least once every year. A physician is a— A banker ... B teacher ... C doctor ... D lawyer.

12 We were cautious when crossing the street. Cautious means— F careful … G unconcerned …H afraid …J worried.

Now turn to page 81. Look at Sample B.

In this part of the test, you will choose words and phrases that best answer questions about paragraphs and stories that you hear. I will read a story and then ask a question. You will choose the best answer to the question. Listen carefully. Mike's mom took him and his little brother to the library. They saw some of their friends there. Together they watched a puppet show. Mike and his brother had a great time.

Now look at Sample B. Listen carefully. Mike and his family went to the— A park ...B museum ... C store ...D library. Darken the circle for the correct answer.

You should have darkened the circle for D, library, because the first sentence of the story says that Mike's mom took Mike and his little brother to the library.

Now you will choose more words and phrases that best answer questions. We will do numbers 13 through 23. Listen carefully to the story and question. Then darken the circle for the correct answer.

Now find number 13. Listen carefully as I read this story. You will answer two questions.

Miss Matay's class put on a play. Cara played a princess. Lori played an evil queen who was jealous of the princess. Tony played a prince who comes to save the princess. "You have the best part in the play," Miss Matay told Vinnie. "You get to play the part of the dragon."

13 Miss Matay's class put on a— A play ...
    B costume ... C mask ...D race.
14 Tony played the part of the—F dragon ...
    G evil queen ...H prince ...J princess.

Now find number 15. Listen as I read this story. You will answer two questions.

Mr. Hernandez packed Carmela's suitcase for summer camp. He packed her play clothes, pajamas, robe, and a swimsuit. On the morning of the second day at camp, it rained very hard. Carmela got ready to walk to the camp kitchen for breakfast. She then discovered that her father had forgotten to pack something.

15 Mr. Hernandez forgot to pack Carmela's—
    A raincoat ... B winter coat ...C sweater ...
    D dress.
16 Which of these would be the best title for this passage? F "A Rainy Day" ... G "Fun at Summer Camp" ... H "The Best Breakfast" ...
    J "Carmela's Problem."

Now find number 17. Listen as I read this poem. You will answer one question.

"Silly me," said Samantha Stocks,
"How did I do this?"
Her cat jumped out of her lunch box!

17 Samantha probably felt— A loving ...B foolish ...
    C sad ... D afraid.

Now find number 18. Listen as I read this story. You will answer two questions.

Gloria helps her mother with the housework every day. Before going to school, Gloria makes her bed. After school, she does her homework. Then she helps her mother cook. She takes out the trash. Finally, she washes the dishes after dinner.

18 Before she goes to school, Gloria— F washes the dishes ...G makes her bed ... H walks the dog ...
    J does her homework.
19 How does Gloria help her mother after dinner?
    A Gloria washes the dishes ....B Gloria takes out the trash .... C Gloria makes her bed ....
    D Gloria helps her mother cook.

Now find number 20. Listen as I read these directions. You will answer three questions.

1. First, take the kite out of the package.
2. Second, insert the wooden pieces into the back of the kite.
3. Next, attach the end of a ball of string to the center of the kite.
4. Finally, make a kite's tail from pieces of cloth and attach it to the kite.
5. If you'd like, you can paint or decorate your kite.

20 The reason wooden pieces are attached to the kite is so that— F the kite can fly ...G the kite won't blow away ...H you can decorate the kite ...J you can catch the kite.
21 According to the directions, the kite's tail can be made from pieces of— A tin ...B cloth ...
    C paper ...D wood.

Now find number 22. Listen carefully as I read this story. You will answer two questions.

Many people are concerned about the environment. There are a number of things that you can do to help clean up the environment. You can pick up trash. You can collect and recycle newspapers, cans, and bottles. You can learn about what causes pollution. Of course, it is easier and more fun to do these things with other people.

22 One way to protect the environment is to—
    F throw away more trash ...G learn how to pollute ...H pick up trash ... J do not be concerned about it.
23 One of the things that cannot be recycled is—
    A bottles ...B pollution ...C newspapers ...
    D cans.

Practice Test 4:

Listening, pp. 118–119

(Give your child scratch paper to take notes if needed.)

In this test you will use your listening skills to answer questions. This test is divided into two parts. For each part there is a sample exercise. We will work each sample together. Look at Sample A. In this part of the test, you will choose words that best complete sentences. Listen carefully. I will read part of a sentence and four answer choices. You will find the word or words that best complete the sentence. Keesha felt upbeat after the speaker's positive message. Positive means— A depressing … B encouraging …C frightening …D upsetting.

You should have darkened the circle for B, encouraging, because positive means encouraging.

Now you will choose more words or groups of words that best complete sentences. Find number 1. We will do numbers 1 through 12 just as we did Sample A. Listen carefully to the sentence and the four answer choices. Then darken the circle for the correct answer.

1 There was a tremendous boulder at the cave entrance. Tremendous means— A tiny … B main …C huge … D important.

2 Grandpa was an employee of that company for 20 years. An employee is a— F teenager … G student …H boss … J worker.

3 Carl wants to compose a poem. To compose means to— A excite …B create …C ruin … D scatter.

4 Some ads try to deceive people. To deceive someone is to— F trick them …G help them … H teach them …J harm them.

5 They want to accomplish their goal this week. To accomplish means to— A admire … B achieve …C rest … D discuss.

6 The castle was a magnificent structure. Magnificent means— F common … G surprising …H pretend …J grand.

7 Last summer my family took a vacation. A vacation is a— A birthday …B holiday … C weekday …D school day.

8 Rita will dash to the finish line. To dash means to— F draw a straight line …G wander around …H slide down something …J run very fast.

9 Her baby wore a pink bonnet. A bonnet is a kind of— A dress …B coat …C snowsuit …D hat.

10 Let's avoid a quarrel. A quarrel is a— F bargain … G settlement …H disagreement …J discussion.

11 We looked in the hollow log. Hollow means— A solid …B narrow …C empty …D overflowing.

12 Many people want to live in a country with liberty. Liberty is— F freedom …G slavery … H responsibility …J duty.

Now go to page 119.

Look at Sample B. In this part of the test, you will choose words and phrases that best answer questions about paragraphs and stories that you hear. I will read a story and then ask a question. You will choose the best answer to the question. Listen carefully. Sometimes during heavy thunderstorms, the electricity stops working. One night, during a storm, the lights at Ronald's house went out. Ronald was very nervous. Ronald's father told him not to worry, and went down to the basement.

Now look at Sample B. Listen carefully. Then darken the circle for the correct answer. Ronald's father went to the basement to get a— A hammer … B flashlight …C sandwich …D radio.

You should have darkened the circle for B, flashlight, because Ronald's father went to the basement to get a flashlight so they would be able to see.

Now you will choose more words and phrases that best answer questions to paragraphs and stories that you hear. Find number 13. We will do numbers 13 through 24 just as we did Sample B. Listen carefully to the story and question. Then darken the circle for the correct answer.

Listen as I read this story. You will answer two questions.

After Kenji was born, Grandma came to visit from Japan. She met my new brother Kenji for the first time. Everyone in my family likes Kenji because he is so cute. They talk about him all day. I like him too, but I want my family to like me again. I came first. I am nine years old. I have a lot to talk about. Kenji cannot talk. He just sleeps in his crib or plays in his playpen all day.

13 What would be a good title for this story? A "Sleeping and Playing" …B "Kenji and His Playpen" …C "A Visit from Japan" …D "An Older Brother's Problem."
14 Everyone likes Kenji because he is so— F loud …G tiny …H cute …J smart.

Now put your finger on number 15. Listen carefully as I read this story. You will answer one question.

Manuel told Larry that his turtle could beat Larry's dog in a race. Larry didn't believe him, so they decided to see what would happen. The dog ran very fast, and the turtle crawled very slowly. But just before the dog reached the finish line, he saw another dog and ran off to play with it. The turtle kept crawling until he reached the finish line.

15 The dog didn't finish the race because he— A became tired …B liked the turtle … C stumbled and fell …D ran off to play.

Now put your finger on number 16. Listen carefully as I read this story. You will answer two questions.

Everyone enjoys Whitehall Park. In the mornings, mothers and fathers spend time there, pushing their babies in strollers. During the afternoons, young children play on the swings and slides. In the evenings, older children play baseball.

16 Young children play in Whitehall Park— F never …G in the mornings …H in the evenings …J in the afternoons.
17 Older children use the park to play— A football …B basketball …C tennis …D baseball.

Now put your finger on number 18. Listen carefully as I read this story. You will answer two questions.

Mr. and Mrs. Hiroshi live in Chicago. They are excited because they are going on a trip. First, they will drive their car to the airport. Then they will fly in a plane to California. From there they will sail on a boat to Hawaii. In Hawaii, they will take a helicopter ride to see parts of the islands.

18 Mr. and Mrs. Hiroshi are going on a trip to— F California …G Hawaii …H Chicago … J Texas.
19 The first thing they will do is— A sail on a boat …B ride in a car …C fly in a plane … D take a helicopter ride.

Now put your finger on number 20. Listen carefully as I read this story. You will answer two questions.

Neil and his grandparents went to Vermont this winter. Neil's grandparents took him on a horse-drawn sleigh ride. His cousins took him ice-skating on the pond. They roasted marshmallows in the fireplace. Neil had a good time in Vermont.

20 Neil went to Vermont with his— F grandparents … G parents …H best friends …J aunt and uncle.
21 Neil's grandparents took him— A shopping … B on a sleigh ride …C ice-skating …D to roast marshmallows.

Now put your finger on number 22. Listen carefully as I read this story. You will answer three questions.

Tara and Matthew built a sand castle. They put three towers on their castle. On top of the tallest tower, they put a flag. They put the door on the middle tower. On the smallest tower, they put a window.

22 After building their castle, Tara and Matthew probably felt— F angry …G scared …H proud … J worried.
23 On top of the tallest tower, Tara and Matthew put— A a flag …B a window …C the door … D another tower.
24 Tara and Matthew are playing on the— F floor … G lawn …H beach …J sidewalk.

UNIT ONE
Reading: Test-Taking Strategies

The following strategies will help you do your best on standardized reading tests. These three strategies will assist y in organizing the information needed to successfully answer th questions.

STRATEGY 1

The CHECK AND SEE Strategy

This strategy can be used when a question asks for a fact from the story. The answer to the question is right there in the story. It is not hidden. Some of the same words may be in the story and in the question.

 Check and See will help you answer *remembering information* questions.

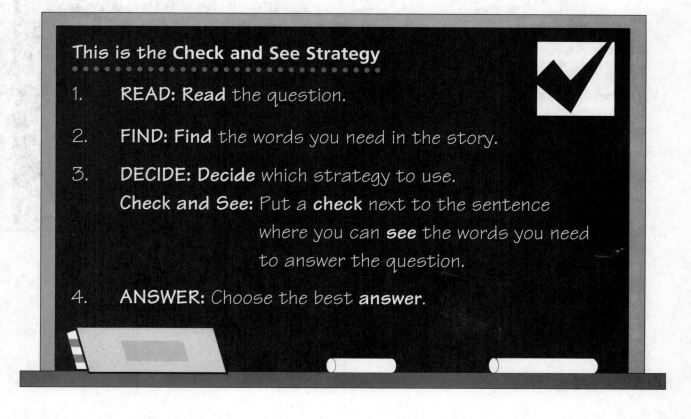

This is the Check and See Strategy

1. READ: **Read** the question.

2. FIND: **Find** the words you need in the story.

3. DECIDE: **Decide** which strategy to use.
    Check and See: Put a **check** next to the sentence where you can **see** the words you need to answer the question.

4. ANSWER: Choose the best **answer**.

GO ON

STRATEGY 2

The PUZZLE PIECE Strategy

This strategy can be used when a question asks you what something means. Sometimes there does not seem to be an answer. It is not stated in the story.

Puzzle Piece is the strategy to use when you must fit facts together to get the answer. This is like putting a puzzle together. Puzzles are made up of many pieces. You cannot look at one piece and know what the picture is. Only when you put the pieces together can you see the whole picture.

This is the Puzzle Piece Strategy

1. **READ: Read** the question.

2. **FIND: Find** the facts you need in the story.

3. **DECIDE: Decide** which strategy to use.
    Write: Write the facts in puzzle pieces.
    Put Together: Put the puzzle pieces **together** to see the picture.

4. **ANSWER:** Choose the best **answer**.

>GO ON>

STRATEGY 3

The WHAT LIGHTS UP Strategy

This is another strategy you can use when an answer is i̶
the story. To answer the question you need to add your o̶
ideas to the story. This added information can come from y̶
own experiences.

 What Lights Up can help you see if something is true, real,
useful, or a fact. It can help you see what would happen if the
story had a different ending.

You can use the **What Lights Up Strategy** to answer the hardest
type of question. This is when you are asked to read and think
of your own ideas. These questions are called *evaluating* and
extending meaning questions.

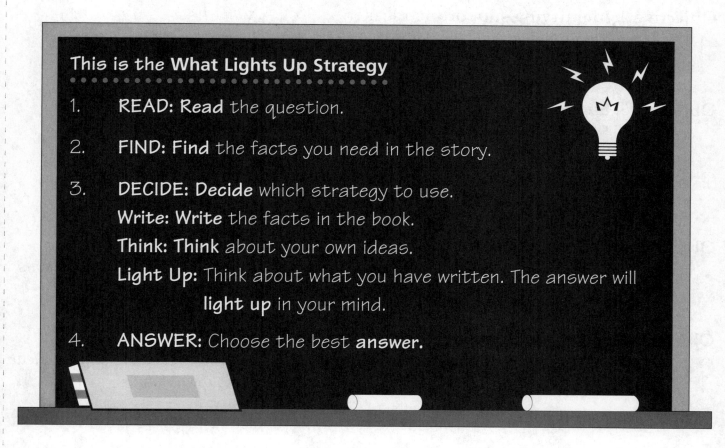

This is the **What Lights Up Strategy**

1.   READ: **Read** the question.

2.   FIND: **Find** the facts you need in the story.

3.   DECIDE: **Decide** which strategy to use.
     Write: **Write** the facts in the book.
     Think: **Think** about your own ideas.
     Light Up: Think about what you have written. The answer will
          light up in your mind.

4.   ANSWER: Choose the best **answer.**

Reading Comprehension

Specific Objectives

Objective 1: Determining word meanings
Prefixes and suffixes, context clues, technical words, and words with multiple meanings

Objective 2: Identifying supporting ideas
Recalling facts and details, sequential order, following directions, and describing settings

Objective 3: Summarizing main ideas
Stated and implied main ideas, and identifying summaries

Objective 4: Perceiving relationships and recognizing outcomes
Cause-and-effect and making predictions

Objective 5: Making inferences and generalizations
Interpreting graphs and diagrams, inferring information, drawing conclusions, making judgments, and evaluating plot

Objective 6: Recognizing points of view, facts, and opinions
Author's purpose, persuasive language, and discerning facts and points of view

Specific Objectives

Objective 1: Determining Word Meanings

Prefixes and suffixes are parts of some words. A *prefix* is at the start of a word. A *suffix* is at the end of a word. You can use prefixes and suffixes to figure out the meaning of a word.

Whenever Shaquana invited a friend to sleep over, she made sure it was someone who liked to stay up late and tell scary stories. Lately, the only books Shaquana liked to read were about the supernatural.

1   In this paragraph, the word supernatural means —

Ⓐ ghosts and spirits.

Ⓑ people who really like nature.

Ⓒ heroes.

Ⓓ strong people.

Hint: Read the entire paragraph. The prefix "super-" means above or greater than normal.

Sometimes having an older sister drives me crazy. She plays her music really loud while I'm doing my homework. If I ask her to turn it down, she'll make it louder.

2   In this paragraph, the word louder means —

Ⓕ quieter.

Ⓖ more than loud.

Ⓗ almost as loud.

Ⓙ almost the same as it was before.

Hint: The suffix "-er" means more than.

Jeff went into his room to find his sneakers. Just as he got near his closet, he found that he was in darkness.

3   What is meant by darkness?

Very dark

Hint: The suffix "-ness" means a state of being.

7

The girls were trying to remember what the new girl at camp was like. Joan said she had brown hair and was skinny. Phyllis thought she was on the tallish side.

4 **In this paragraph, the word tallish means —**

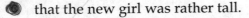

Ⓐ that the new girl talked a lot.

Ⓑ that the new girl was shy.

Ⓒ that the new girl was rather tall.

Ⓓ that the new girl was of Irish background.

Hint: The suffix "-ish" means somewhat or rather.

My mother asked me to get everything ready. She wanted to make dinner for us when she got home. She told me to take the meat out of the refrigerator and preheat the oven. Then she wanted me to start washing the lettuce.

5 **In this paragraph, the word preheat means —**

Ⓕ check the temperature of.

Ⓖ turn on.

Ⓗ heat beforehand.

Ⓙ clean.

Hint: "Pre-" is a prefix. "Pre-" means before.

The boys were planning a garage sale. They had cleaned the toys and found all the pieces for the games. But their old clothes were in such bad shape, they did not think they could resell them.

6 **What does it mean when someone resells something?**

_____

Not selling

_____

_____

_____

_____

Hint: "Re-" is a prefix. "Re-" means to do something again.

GO ON

Objective 1: Determining Word Meanings

Sometimes you can figure out the meaning of a new word by using the words around it as clues.

Sherlock Holmes is a great detective. But he lives only in books. The <u>tales</u> about him have been written in 57 languages.

1   **In this paragraph, the word <u>tales</u> means —**

    Ⓐ   places.

    Ⓑ   names.

    Ⓒ   stories.

    Ⓓ   pens.

Hint: You get a clue as to what the word <u>tales</u> means by reading sentences 2 and 3.

Marie did not know how to operate the compact disc player. She read the <u>manual</u>. She hoped she could find the information she needed in the book.

2   **In this paragraph, the word <u>manual</u> means —**

    Ⓕ   a dictionary.

    Ⓖ   a compact disc.

    Ⓗ   a recipe book.

    Ⓙ   a how-to book.

Hint: You get a clue as to what the word <u>manual</u> means from the sentence after the one in which the word appears.

Mother ducks often take their <u>ducklings</u> swimming. When a pond is full of mothers and babies, the mother ducks quack and swim around. Whichever mother duck quacks the loudest gets the greatest number of ducklings to swim around her.

3   **What are <u>ducklings</u>?**

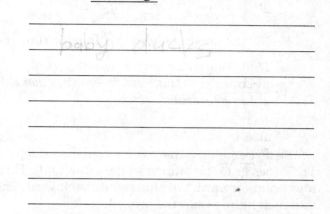

baby ducks

Hint: You get a clue as to what the word <u>ducklings</u> means from the second sentence in the paragraph.

 GO ON

Pat grew up wanting to be a postmaster. As a boy, whenever he went to the post office in his home town in Ohio, he would dream of running it. When he finished school, his dream almost came true. He became a postmaster, but in a different town in Ohio.

4   **In this paragraph, the word postmaster means —**

Ⓐ   someone who likes to collect stamps.

Ⓑ   an expert about postage.

Ⓒ   a person in charge of a post office.

Ⓓ   the person who posts time for runners.

Hint: You get a clue as to what the word postmaster means from the sentence that tells about Pat's dream.

Birds perch on a tree even while they sleep. Their toes grab the branch so they don't fall. Three toes point forward. One toe points backward. The toes lock tightly onto the branch.

5   **In this paragraph, the word perch means —**

Ⓕ   fly.

Ⓖ   sit.

Ⓗ   vanish.

Ⓙ   promise.

Hint: You get a clue as to what the word perch means by reading the sentences after the one in which the word appears.

Doctors studied thousands of people. Some of the people spent a lot of time alone. Many of these people had weak hearts. They were more likely to have a heart attack. Other people spent a lot of time with their families and friends. Most of these social people had strong hearts.

6   **Describe someone who is social.**

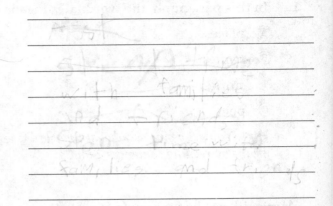

Hint: You get a clue as to what the word social means by reading the sentence before the word.

Objective 1: Determining Word Meanings

Specialized or technical words are used in science and social studies. You can use the other information in the passage to help figure out the meaning of these words.

Sometimes, deep in the ocean, an earthquake shakes the ocean floor. The movement starts a <u>tidal wave</u>. At first, the wave is small. But it can move toward the shore at a speed of up to 500 miles per hour. By the time it reaches the coast, it is huge and hits hard.

1 **In this paragraph, <u>tidal wave</u> means —**

- Ⓐ a way of saying hello.

- Ⓑ a very big wave sent to shore by an earthquake.

- Ⓒ a strong gust of wind.

- Ⓓ a group of people that stands up and down in a stadium.

Hint: <u>Tidal wave</u> *is a technical word. You get a clue as to what it means by reading the entire paragraph.*

There are giant ships more than 700 feet long. These ships were built to carry tons of wheat from place to place. They have a ramp folded up in back. When they get to shore, the ramp unfolds. The <u>cargo</u> is moved off the ship by the ramp.

2 **In this paragraph, the word <u>cargo</u> means —**

- Ⓕ truck.

- Ⓖ garbage.

- Ⓗ shipment.

- Ⓙ flower.

Hint: <u>Cargo</u> *is a technical word. You get a clue as to what it means by reading the sentences before the word.*

<u>Saliva</u> helps you swallow food by making your throat slippery. Saliva softens food so that the tongue can taste it. <u>Saliva</u> also helps your body break down food.

3 **What is <u>saliva</u> and where do you find it?**

Spit and you is in your Mouth

Hint: <u>Saliva</u> *is a technical word. You can get a clue as to what it means by reading the entire paragraph.*

▶GO ON▶

Wildflowers grow in many <u>environments</u>. Some are found in woods or fields. Others grow on mountains or in streams and ponds. Wildflowers can grow in the desert, too.

4 **In this paragraph, the word <u>environments</u> means —**

Ⓐ blossoms.

Ⓑ settings.

Ⓒ oceans.

Ⓓ insects.

Hint: You get a clue as to what <u>environments</u> means from the sentences after the word.

Ted couldn't believe that he was on a real television <u>set</u>. Carpenters were working all around him building the scenes where the action would take place. Some painters were working on the rooms of a house, and others were painting a yard. He hoped his parents would let him stay long enough to meet one of the actors or actresses.

5 **In this paragraph, the word <u>set</u> means —**

Ⓕ a number of tools that are used together.

Ⓖ the number of couples needed for a square dance.

Ⓗ a group of tennis games.

Ⓙ a place where a show is filmed.

Hint: <u>Set</u> is a technical word. You get a clue as to what it means by reading the entire paragraph.

Piranhas are fish. They live in South American waters. These fish tend to swim in large groups. They will tear the flesh off an animal or person that is in the water. In just minutes, all that is left is the <u>skeleton</u>.

6 **What is a <u>skeleton</u>?**

A persons or animals bones

Hint: <u>Skeleton</u> is a technical word. You get a clue as to what it means by reading the sentence before the word.

STOP

Objective 2: Identifying Supporting Ideas

Facts or details are important. By noticing them, you will know what the passage is about.

The United States Supreme Court is the highest court of the land. For many years, only men were Supreme Court judges. That was true until 1981. That year, Sandra Day O'Connor became a Supreme Court judge. She was the first woman to do so.

Sandra's first teacher was her mother. Later, Sandra went to school. Sandra finished high school when she was just 16. Then, she followed her dream to study law. She was in law school for five years. When she finished law school, she couldn't find a job. Very few companies wanted women lawyers!

1 **Only men served on the Supreme Court —**

(A) after 1990.

(B) after 1811.

(C) until 1981.

(D) until 200 years ago.

Hint: Look at sentences 2 and 3.

2 **The highest court of the United States is the —**

(F) World Court.

(G) State Court.

(H) Supreme Court.

(J) Day Court.

Hint: Look for this sentence in the passage.

3 **What was Sandra's dream?**

To study law

Hint: Look at sentence 9.

Sandra married a man she met in law school. They both got jobs as lawyers. For a while, Sandra had her own law office. Then, she and her husband had a son. Sandra decided to stay home. Sandra and her husband had two more sons.

After nine years, Sandra became a judge in Arizona. She was a judge there for seven years. Then, one of the judges from the Supreme Court left. So the Supreme Court needed another judge. The President of the United States heard about Sandra. He asked her to become a judge on the Supreme Court. She eagerly said, "Yes!"

4 **The President asked Sandra Day O'Connor to be a —**

Ⓐ student at a university.

Ⓑ lawyer in Arizona.

Ⓒ judge in an Arizona court.

Ⓓ judge on the Supreme Court.

Hint: Find the section that talks about the President.

5 **Sandra had —**

Ⓕ three sons.

Ⓖ two daughters.

Ⓗ a son and a daughter.

Ⓙ four children.

Hint: Count the number of sons mentioned in the passage.

6 **Sandra and her husband were both —**

Ⓐ doctors.

Ⓑ lawyers.

Ⓒ teachers.

Ⓓ bankers.

Hint: Look at sentence 2.

7 **How long did Sandra stay home with her children?**

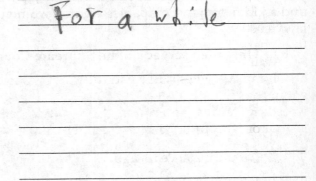

For a while

Hint: Look at sentence 7.

▶ GO ON ▶

Objective 2: Identifying Supporting Ideas

It is helpful to put events in the order they happened. This may help you to understand a passage.

Long, long ago, the ancient Greeks served a god named Zeus. They honored Zeus by giving grand festivals. The festivals were held in a place called Olympia. During the festivals, athletes showed their strength and speed. These festivals were the first Olympic Games.

In the year 776 B.C., the 200-meter race was won by a young man named Coroebus. He is the first Olympic winner on record. The next festival took place in 772 B.C. This time the Greeks wanted to offer more to their god. So, they held new sporting events. Many people came to watch them. For the next 1,000 years, the Olympics were held every four years. They always took place in Olympia.

At first, only people with money could afford to be Olympic athletes. They had the time to train and get in shape. Some of the events were horse racing, wrestling, boxing, and running. The first Olympics lasted for five days. Prizes were given on the last day. Winning was the most important part of athletics for the ancient Greeks. The winners marched in a parade toward the Temple of Zeus. Along the way, crowds tossed flowers at them. The winners wore olive wreaths. The Greeks gave prizes to the first-place winners only. People teased the losers.

The games were stopped in A.D. 393. At that time, the Romans ruled Greece. The emperor did not like the Greek gods. So, he stopped the Olympic events. The Greek temples stood empty. Over the years, they were buried by floods and earthquakes. In 1892, a Frenchman wanted to start the Olympic Games once again. He thought that the games would bring the people of the world together in peace. In 1896, he succeeded. The first modern games were held in Athens, Greece.

1   **When did the Olympic festivals stop?**

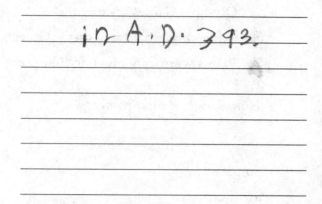

in A.D. 393.

Hint: Look at the last paragraph.

2 **When were prizes given?**

Ⓐ on the first day

Ⓑ after each event

Ⓒ on the fifth day

Ⓓ every day

Hint: Look at the section mentioning the prizes.

3 **Which of these events happened last in the story?**

Ⓔ Coroebus won a race in Olympia.

Ⓕ A Frenchman wanted to start the Olympic Games once again.

Ⓖ Games were held in Athens, Greece.

Ⓗ Prizes were only given to first-place winners.

Hint: Look at the last paragraph.

4 **Which of these happened first in the story?**

Ⓐ The Greeks held a festival in 772 B.C.

Ⓑ The Roman emperor stopped the games in Olympia.

Ⓒ The Greeks held a festival in 776 B.C.

Ⓓ Some events were horse racing, wrestling, boxing, and running.

Hint: Look at the beginning of the story.

5 **When were the first modern Olympic games held?**

_____

_____

_____

_____

_____

_____

Hint: Look at the section about the modern Olympics.

GO ON

Objective 2: Identifying Supporting Ideas

Written directions tell you how to do something. Every step is important.

My friend told me to meet her at her mother's office at 3 P.M. She told me to walk to building #120 on Liberty Street and then to go in the main entrance and down the flight of stairs on the left. Then, I should turn left at the bottom of the stairs and go down the hall to office #3B. She will be waiting for me inside the office.

1 To get to my friend's mother's office, I should first —

Ⓐ take a bus.

Ⓑ take the elevator right inside the main entrance.

Ⓒ turn right at the bottom of the stairs.

Ⓓ go to #120 Liberty Street.

Hint: Read the directions. They start with the second sentence.

Do the lights ever go out in your neighborhood? They do in ours a lot. Sometimes they go out when it is very hot and everyone is using their air conditioners. Other times, it is during a storm. Luckily, I know what to do when the lights go out. First, I get our flashlight. Then, I go around the house turning off all the lights that were on before, as well as the television and clothes dryer. Next, I call the electric company to find out what's going on. Then I go back to reading my book—using the flashlight!

2 What is the first thing you should do if the lights go out in your house?

_____

_____

_____

_____

_____

_____

_____

Hint: Read the directions. They start with the word "first."

I do not like cooking. I do enjoy baking. I think that it is a lot of fun to bake a cake for a party. My favorite cake is plain yellow, because then I can put any kind of icing on it. Here is the recipe:

Step 1: Make a list of all the things you need to get at the store to make the cake.

Step 2: When you have everything, measure the right amount of water.

Step 3: Mix the water with the cake mix and two eggs.

Step 4: Bake it in the oven for about thirty minutes.

Step 5: Take the cake out of the oven and let it cool.

Step 6: Ice the cake with any flavor you like: vanilla, chocolate, or strawberry.

3   When do you put the cake in the oven?

Ⓕ   Step 2

Ⓖ   Step 3

Ⓗ   Step 4

Ⓙ   Step 5

Hint: Read the steps in order, starting with Step 1.

4   Before you start to make a cake, you should —

Ⓐ   mix the water with the eggs.

Ⓑ   mix the cake mix with the eggs.

Ⓒ   make sure you have all the ingredients you need.

Ⓓ   take the top off the can of icing you bought at the store.

Hint: Read the steps in order, starting with Step 1.

5   What should you do right after you bake the cake?

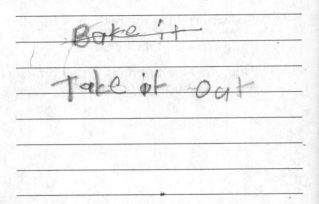

Bake it

Take it out

Hint: Read the steps starting with Step 4.

GO ON ▶

Objective 2: Identifying Supporting Ideas

The setting of a story lets you know when and where the story is taking place.

Richard Byrd stood outside the small cabin on March 28, 1934. He shook hands with the men who were leaving. They were heading back to the main camp on the east coast of Antarctica. He would stay at the base camp for the winter. There was plenty of food and fuel in the tiny cabin. He felt sure nothing would go wrong.

But something did go wrong. Byrd was burning kerosene for heat, and the fumes were poisoning him. He continued to make his radio messages, because he didn't want anyone to try to rescue him in the dangerous weather. Byrd managed to stay alive until August, when three men arrived at the base camp. They hardly recognized Byrd. He was very thin and looked terrible. Byrd greeted them and then fell to the ground. The men had arrived in the nick of time. After two months of care, Byrd's good health returned.

1   The story takes place —

Ⓐ 100 years ago.

Ⓑ within the past 25 years.

Ⓒ over 60 years ago.

Ⓓ in 1943.

Hint: Read the first sentence.

2   The story takes place —

Ⓕ at the main camp.

Ⓖ on the coast of Antarctica.

Ⓗ in a large cabin.

Ⓙ at the base camp.

Hint: Read the first paragraph.

3   When was Richard Byrd rescued?

the nick of time.

Hint: Find the section that talks about Byrd's rescue.

The strongest earthquake in the United States happened in Missouri. It took place in 1811. The center of the earthquake was near a town called New Madrid. Since few people lived near this town, nobody was killed. But the earthquake was quite strong. It changed the course of the Mississippi River.

4   When did the earthquake occur?

- Ⓐ in 1911
- Ⓑ in 1918
- Ⓒ in 1811
- Ⓓ in 1981

Hint: Look at the second sentence.

5   Where was the earthquake?

In the United States in Missoury.

Hint: Read the first three sentences.

Going to the horse show on that beautiful summer day was a great experience. Before the events started, we were able to get very close to the riders and their horses. Then, after we found our seats, we spent the afternoon watching each rider and horse perform. At the end of the day, the best performers were given ribbons and prizes.

6   When is this story taking place?

- Ⓕ in the summer
- Ⓖ in the spring
- Ⓗ at night
- Ⓙ in the morning

Hint: Look at the first sentence.

STOP

Objective 3: Summarizing Main Ideas

The main idea is the meaning of a passage. Many times it is a sentence in the passage.

A chameleon is a kind of lizard. Its skin is clear, but it can change color. Under its skin are layers of cells. These cells have yellow, black, and red color in them. Anger makes these colors darken. Fear makes them lighten. It also makes yellow spots appear. Temperature and light can also cause the colors to change. These changes make the chameleon hard to see. Changing colors can save a chameleon's life.

1   What is the main idea of this story?

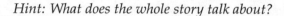

Chameleon's can cha
nge colors

Hint: What does the whole story talk about?

Don't worry if there are times when you get angry. Getting angry can be both good and bad. Many doctors think that it's all right to show your anger sometimes. People who get angry once in a while may live happier lives. But people must be careful when they are angry. Angry people don't always think clearly. They can do things that they may be sorry about later.

2   What is the main idea of this story?

Ⓐ People can't think straight when they are angry.

Ⓑ People get angry about nothing.

Ⓒ Anger can be both good and bad.

Ⓓ Anger can make you sick.

Hint: Which choice sums up the whole passage?

John Chapman planted apple trees in Ohio in the early 1800s. He carried the seeds all over the country. He sold the seeds or just gave them away to people. Chapman was a very kind man. He loved people, animals, and trees. The story of Johnny Appleseed is the story of his life.

3   What is the main idea of this story?

Ⓕ Apple trees grow from seeds.

Ⓖ We get the story of Johnny Appleseed from the life of John Chapman.

Ⓗ John Chapman lived in Ohio.

Ⓙ John Chapman traveled the country.

Hint: What does the whole story talk about?

Sometimes, people need help when they get older. Older people may need help walking or cooking food. At night, they count on their families to do these things for them. But during the day, they may be left at home alone. To help them, some cities have built day-care centers. Older people can go to these centers during the day. There they will get the help they need.

4   What is the main idea of this story?

Ⓐ Older people can get the help they need in day-care centers.

Ⓑ Older people cook their lunch.

Ⓒ Families are busy at night.

Ⓓ Older people need help walking.

Hint: All of the sentences in the paragraph give you the main idea.

A man in Florida can talk to fish. He spent a long time learning how to do this. First, he watched fish very closely. Then, he listened to the noises they made. Finally, he learned to make the same sounds. Sometimes, the fish listen to him. At times he can even make them do things. This man thinks that someday fishermen might be able to call fish to their nets.

5   What is the main idea of this story?

Ⓕ Some fish listen to sounds.

Ⓖ Many people like to fish.

Ⓗ Fish never listen.

Ⓙ A man in Florida talks to fish.

Hint: What does the whole story talk about?

▶ GO ON ▶

Objective 3: Summarizing Main Ideas

A good summary contains the main idea of a passage. It is short but includes the most important points.

One kind of spider makes a web underwater. It weaves its web in water plants. Then, it carries bubbles of air down to fill the web. The water spider lies still on its web. Soon, a water insect swims near it. The spider dashes out and catches the insect. It brings its catch back to the air-filled web to eat.

1 **Which sentence tells what this story is mostly about?**

Ⓐ Some spiders look better underwater.

Ⓑ Water spiders build their webs using air bubbles.

Ⓒ Water spiders like water insects.

Ⓓ One kind of spider can live underwater very well.

Hint: Which sentence tells you about the whole passage?

It is hard to think of doctors as artists. But their job of healing people can be beautiful. For instance, doctors help people who can't hear well. In some cases, doctors use a piece of a rib. They carve the rib so that it fits inside the ear. The bone is about a tenth of an inch high. It also has a pretty and interesting shape. With this bone in the ear, the person can hear much better.

2 **What is the best summary of this passage?**

Ⓕ Some people think that a doctor is a kind of artist because healing people is beautiful.

Ⓖ People who can't hear well need to use their ribs to try to hear better.

Ⓗ Artists know how to carve ribs into pretty shapes.

Ⓙ Doctors help artists hear better using pieces of ribs.

Hint: Which sentence tells you about the whole passage?

GO ON

Calamity Jane was a famous woman of the Wild West. She was famous because she was so tough. She lived during the 1800s. She learned to ride a horse and shoot a gun at an early age. People could always hear her coming. She also liked to dress in men's clothes. There weren't many women like her.

3   What is this story mostly about?

Ⓐ It was tough for Calamity Jane to live during the 1800s.

Ⓑ Calamity Jane was famous because she was taught to ride a horse.

Ⓒ Calamity Jane did things that other women in the 1800s did not.

Ⓓ Calamity Jane wore men's clothes.

Hint: Which sentence sums up Calamity Jane?

Cats are very much like lions and tigers. They can jump high in the air. Cats can jump seven feet high. They have padded feet. That way they can sneak up on their prey. Cats have 18 claws on their feet. They can push out and draw back their claws.

4   What is this story mostly about?

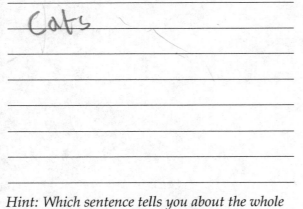

Cats

Hint: Which sentence tells you about the whole passage?

Two things make a tree a conifer. One is that it must make seeds in its cones. It must also have needle-like leaves. Conifers are called evergreen trees. They look green all the time. Conifers do lose and replace their leaves. But they never lose all their leaves at the same time.

5   What is this story mostly about?

Trees

Hint: Which sentence tells you about the whole paragraph?

STOP

Objective 4: Perceiving Relationships and Recognizing Outcomes

Knowing what happened (effect) and what made it happen (cause) helps you to understand what you read.

The big dance was Friday night, and Jodi needed a dress to wear. As she was sorting through her closet, her older sister, Gabriela, tapped her on the shoulder. She knew that Jodi had always liked her blue dress. "How would you like to wear this?" she asked. Jodi's eyes lit up. She hugged Gabriela and ran to try on the dress.

1 Why was Jodi happy?

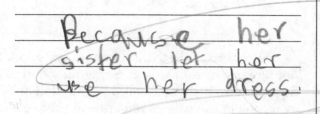

Because her sister let her use her dress.

Hint: Jodi's eyes lighting up is the effect. What made this happen?

2 Why did Jodi need a dress to wear?

Ⓐ She wanted to be like her older sister, Gabriela.

Ⓑ The big dance was Friday night.

Ⓒ She was tired of blue dresses in her closet.

Ⓓ She couldn't find any dresses in her closet.

Hint: Jodi needing a dress is the effect. What made this happen?

Alex and Vince were spending a week at camp. Tonight was their last night, and it was "skit night." The campers in each cabin had written plays about their camp experiences. Alex had seen how easily Vince made friends with everyone in the camp. When Vince was chosen to be the announcer for skit night, Alex dumped a box of cookie crumbs in Vince's sleeping bag.

3 **Why did the campers write plays about their camp experiences?**

(F) They liked to write plays.

(G) They had so much fun at camp that they had a lot to write about.

(H) They were going to put on skits.

(J) Their camp counselors asked them to write plays.

Hint: Writing plays is the effect. What made this happen?

4 **Why did Alex dump a box of cookie crumbs in Vince's sleeping bag?**

(A) Vince was chosen to be the announcer for skit night.

(B) Alex knew how much his friend liked cookies.

(C) Alex wanted to have a party in the cabin after skit night.

(D) Vince needed more cookies because he had so many friends.

Hint: Alex dumping a box of cookies in Vince's sleeping bag is the effect. What made this happen?

5 **Why was Vince chosen as the announcer for skit night?**

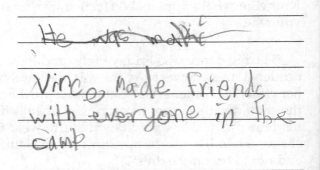

He was not the

Vince made friends with everyone in the camp

Hint: Being chosen as announcer is the effect. What made this happen?

Trena's baseball team was not very good. It had not won a game all season. Something had to be done, or else the team would be laughed at by everyone in town. So, Trena promised to eat one bug for every run the team scored. That night, the team scored twenty runs and finally won a game.

6 **Why hadn't Trena's baseball team won a game all season?**

(F) Everyone in town laughed at the team.

(G) The team ate bugs and got sick.

(H) The team was not very good.

(J) Something interrupted practices.

Hint: Not winning a game is the effect. What made this happen?

7 **Why did the team score twenty runs?**

(A) They ate bugs before the game.

(B) They had many fans in town.

(C) There were twenty girls on the team.

(D) Trena had promised to eat one bug for every run scored.

Hint: Scoring twenty runs is the effect. What made this happen?

Objective 4: Perceiving Relationships and Recognizing Outcomes

Many times you can tell in advance what is probably going to happen next. You must think about what would make sense if the story were to go on.

In the morning, Becky came downstairs. "I don't like this house at all," the girl told her parents. "It smells funny." Her mother asked if she had seen the wild strawberries growing in the front yard. Her father mentioned the pony he had seen at the neighboring house. The girl's eyes lit up.

1   What will Becky probably do?

Ⓐ The family will sell the house and move because of the smell.

Ⓑ The father will buy the pony for Becky.

Ⓒ Becky will find some things she likes about that house.

Ⓓ Becky will get angry because her eyes have lit up.

Hint: Think about how Becky feels at the end of the story, before you make your choice.

The man was trying to balance himself. His bicycle was picking up speed on the steep hill. He hit a bump, and one foot lost its grip on the pedal.

2   What will probably happen next?

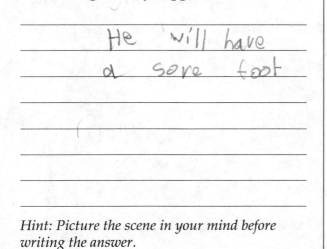

He will have a sore foot

Hint: Picture the scene in your mind before writing the answer.

The shaggy animal went up to the back door. It rattled the screen door with its front paw and then sat down. It was quiet for a while. But soon a face appeared at the door, and then there was a scream of joy. "It's Goldie!" a girl's voice said. "She's come back."

3   What will the girl probably do next?

Ⓕ run to get her mother

Ⓖ open the door to let Goldie in

Ⓗ shut and lock the inside door

Ⓙ scream again

Hint: What is most likely to happen next?

Valentina Tereshkova was nervous. She knew she'd soon make history. It was a still morning. She sat strapped in her seat. At last, the Soviet spaceship began to shake. Its great engines roared. The ship climbed from the launch pad. It built up speed. Soon, it was racing through the sky. Valentina had become the first woman in space.

4   What will Valentina probably do next?

Ⓐ   call her mother

Ⓑ   have lunch

Ⓒ   follow the steps she was trained to do in space

Ⓓ   rest so that she could think clearly

Hint: What seems most likely to happen based on all the sentences?

Cris looked at the window to make sure it was open. Then she marked her place and closed the book. She put it on the table next to her bed. Then she fluffed up the pillow and set the alarm clock.

5   What will Cris most likely do next?

Ⓕ   fall asleep

Ⓖ   have a snack

Ⓗ   get into bed

Ⓙ   take a shower

Hint: Read the entire paragraph.

When Sammy woke up, he looked out the window. The slopes were covered with snow. Quickly, he pulled on his long underwear and other warm clothes. He ate a good, hot breakfast so that he'd have plenty of energy. Then he checked his equipment. He walked in his heavy boots toward the door.

6   What is probably going to happen next?

Ⓐ   Sammy is going to ski down the slopes.

Ⓑ   Sammy is going ice skating.

Ⓒ   Sammy is going to play golf.

Ⓓ   Sammy is going to stay inside.

Hint: You need to read the whole paragraph, but especially the last sentence.

STOP

Objective 5: Making Inferences and Generalizations

The way a character acts tells you about that person's mood.

Al had been standing in line at the counter waiting to pay for the things he had chosen. The store was hot, and the air conditioning didn't work. Al was holding some heavy objects, and he wished the line would move faster. A woman cut to the front of the line. People protested, but the woman didn't budge. Suddenly, Al threw his things into a nearby cart and walked quickly out of the store.

1 **How was Al feeling when he left the store?**

Ⓐ Al had gotten tired of waiting and planned to come back when the store wasn't so busy.

Ⓑ Al was hungry and looking forward to lunch.

Ⓒ Al was angry that he had waited so long only to have someone cut into the line.

Ⓓ Al felt that he had chosen the wrong items.

Hint: Carefully think about the entire passage, especially the last sentence.

Ian and Louise were supposed to be planting corn, beans, and carrots together. While Louise dug up the old garden and turned over the soil, Ian sat under a tree sipping a cool drink. While Louise dug in fertilizer and raked the garden, Ian ate his lunch. When the soil was finally ready for the seeds to be planted, Ian said to Louise, "I'll plant the seeds." Louise yelled back, "No, thanks! I'll plant the seeds!"

2 **How did Louise feel?**

good

_____

_____

_____

_____

_____

_____

Hint: You must read the entire passage and what Louise said at the end of the story to find out how Louise felt.

When the baby came home from the hospital, his five-year-old brother, Mike, shouted, "Take it back! You got a new baby because I'm not good enough for you!" Mike's parents talked with him for a long time. They told him that the baby would need special care at first. But that didn't mean they didn't love Mike anymore.

3   How did Mike feel about his new baby brother?

F   Mike was mad because the baby cried all the time.

G   Mike was mad because he didn't want to take care of the baby.

H   Mike felt his parents loved the new baby more than they loved him.

J   Mike felt that the baby should not get special care.

Hint: Read what Mike said to discover how he felt.

A fisherman brought a large fish to the king and was paid well for it. As the fisherman left, he picked up a valuable coin from the floor. The angry king called to him, "That is not yours." The man answered, "I did not want someone to step on the king's face. That is why I picked up the coin." The king smiled and let the man keep the coin.

4   How did the king feel after the man said something?

happy

Hint: Carefully think about the entire passage, especially what the king did at the end of the passage.

STOP

Objective 6: Recognizing Points of View, Facts, and Opinions

It is important to know the difference between fact and opinion. A fact is real and true. An opinion is a feeling or belief. Words that describe are used to offer opinions.

Stephen Hawking is a famous scientist. He has written books about physics and our universe. But Hawking must do all his work in a wheelchair. In his twenties, he found out that he had Lou Gehrig's disease. Later, he lost his power to speak and write. Now, he does all his work on a special computer. The computer allows him to speak.

1   **Why does Stephen Hawking use a computer?**

He lost his power to speak and write

Hint: A fact is real and true. What is said in the passage?

A sun dog is a bright ring around the sun. Sometimes, the sun dog will also have colors. It may look like a round rainbow. Sun dogs are caused by ice crystals high in the sky. You should never look right at the sun. So wear sunglasses if you want to see a sun dog.

2   **Which of these is an OPINION from the passage?**

Ⓐ   A sun dog is caused by ice crystals.

Ⓑ   You should not look right at the sun.

Ⓒ   The rainbow colors of a sun dog are beautiful.

Ⓓ   A sun dog is a bright ring around the sun.

Hint: Words that describe are opinion words.

>GO ON▶

Did you know that your body shrinks as the day goes by? When you wake up, you are at your tallest. Your body is relaxed. Your muscles are stretched, and your joints are loose. As the day passes, your muscles tighten. Gravity pulls down on your body, too. Your body may be an inch shorter by the end of the day.

3   Which of these is a FACT from the passage?

(F)   When you wake up, you feel good because your body is relaxed.

(G)   It is good that your muscles tighten so that you don't fall down.

(H)   Gravity pulls down on your body.

(J)   It's better to be short than tall.

Hint: Words like "feel good," "it is good," and "it is better" are opinion words.

Have you ever watched a pond freeze in winter? The water freezes first on the top. The ice forms a very thin sheet across the water. It takes only about twenty minutes for this sheet to form. Then slowly the ice begins to grow down toward the bottom. It takes an hour for the first sheet to become two times as thick as it was when it started.

4   Which of these is NOT a fact from the passage?

(A)   When ice freezes it looks pretty.

(B)   It takes about twenty minutes for the first sheet of ice to form.

(C)   It takes an hour for the first sheet to become two times as thick.

(D)   Ice freezes first on top, forming a very thin sheet across the water.

Hint: Facts are real and true. Which sentence is an opinion?

For years, traveling farm workers were not treated well. At last, Cesar Chavez could stand it no longer. He thought farm workers should be paid more. He wanted better working conditions for them. To gain these, he formed a union. The group went on strike to get what they wanted.

5   Which of these is a FACT from the passage?

(F)   It was not fair that farm workers were not treated well.

(G)   Better working conditions mean that farm workers will produce more.

(H)   To gain better working conditions, Cesar Chavez formed a union.

(J)   It is not a good idea to go on strike.

Hint: A fact is real and true. What is actually said in the passage?

Reading Selections

Directions: Read each story carefully. Then read each question. Darken the circle for the correct answer, or write in the answer.

> **TRY THIS** More than one answer choice may seem correct. Choose the answer that goes best with the story.

Sample A   **Our Pancakes**

Dad and I made our own breakfast. We made pancakes. They tasted better than Mom's pancakes. Dad and I decided we would keep this as our little secret.

Why will they keep the secret?

Ⓐ They do not want Mom to know they cooked breakfast. ✓

Ⓑ They do not want to hurt Mom's feelings.

Ⓒ They burned the pancakes.

Ⓓ They want to make breakfast again next week.

> **THINK IT THROUGH** The correct answer is **B, They do not want to hurt Mom's feelings**. The story states that the pancakes tasted better than Mom's pancakes, but they will keep this secret rather than hurt Mom's feelings.

STOP

Jill and Jo

Jill and Jo were playing. Jo ran to hide. Jill looked for her. Then it began to rain. Jill and Jo got wet. They ran to the house.

1 **What were the girls playing?**

Hide and go seek

2 **Why did Jill and Jo run to the house?**

Ⓐ because they were tired

Ⓑ because it was hot

Ⓒ because it was raining ✓

Ⓓ because it was time for lunch

The Girls Get Lost!

Sheila used to live in a large city where she had many friends. When her mother got a job in a small town, Sheila was upset. She didn't want to move. She didn't want to leave her friends, especially her best friend, Katie. Sheila's mother promised that they would arrange a visit with Katie soon.

One day Sheila's mother asked her, "How would you like to go to the zoo on Saturday? I just talked to Mrs. Lee on the phone. She and Katie can meet us there." Sheila was excited. She couldn't think of anything she'd rather do.

The next Saturday was cold and clear. Sheila put on many layers of warm clothing. She had made a book for Katie. It told all about the fun things they had done when they lived next door to each other.

When Sheila and her mother drove up to the zoo, they saw Katie and her mother waiting at the entrance. Sheila and Katie were glad to see each other. They hurried down the path to the monkey house. "Wait for us there," Mrs. Lee said. But the girls were so busy talking that they didn't even hear her.

The girls watched the gorillas for a while. They had never seen such large apes. Then they ran to the area with lions and tigers.

They bought some food for the elephants and fed them. They spent a long time watching a giraffe and its baby.

When they started getting hungry, they turned around to look for their mothers, but they couldn't find them anywhere. "Uh oh! I think we might be in trouble," Sheila said. Katie was worried, too. The girls sat down and tried to think of what to do.

They decided to follow the signs back to the entrance.

When they had walked a long time, they saw their mothers. Their mothers were happy to see them. They had been worried about the girls. "Where have you been? We've been looking everywhere for you!" Sheila's mother said. The girls didn't know what to say. Later Katie whispered to Sheila. "Well, I guess we can add another chapter to the book you wrote. We can write about the time we got lost at the zoo."

GO ON

3 The boxes below show events that happened in the story.

The girls met at the zoo.	T ~~The drops to the zoo~~	The girls fed the elephants.
1	**2**	**3**

What belongs in the second box?

F The girls watched a giraffe.

G The girls started getting hungry.

(H) The girls watched the gorillas. ✓

J The girls found their mothers.

4 Which question does the first paragraph answer?

(A) Why was Sheila upset? ✓

B What is the name of the small town where Sheila moved?

C How did the girls get lost?

D What is Katie's favorite food?

5 Why were the mothers upset?

They ~~coulcou~~ couldn't find their
Daughters couldn't
find their
daughters

6 What is this story **mainly** about?

F Sheila's move to a small town

(G) Sheila's mother's new job

(H) the monkey house

J the girls' day at the zoo ✓

7 Why did Mrs. Lee tell the girls to wait for their mothers at the monkey house?

A She liked monkeys.

(B) She did not want the girls to get lost.

C She was cold.

D She was talking to Sheila's mother.

8 What was the weather like on the day the girls visited the zoo?

F hot

G cold and cloudy

H rainy

(J) cold and clear ✓

9 A gorilla is a—

A type of lion.

B type of fish.

C kind of elephant.

(D) large ape. ✓

GO ON

Making a Clay Pot

With practice, anyone can make a simple pot from clay. Take a piece of clay the size of an apple, and put it on a flat surface. Press and squeeze it until there are no lumps or air bubbles. Then, using both hands, shape the clay into a smooth, round ball.

Now you are ready to begin. Keep the ball in your left hand. With the thumb of your right hand, make an opening in the clay. Press down toward your palm, leaving one half inch of clay at the bottom. This will be the base of your pot. Now keep your thumb inside the pot. Press the clay gently between your thumb and fingers. Turn the pot after each squeeze. This will make the pot thin out evenly. Continue squeezing and turning until the pot is as thin as you want it.

Now the pot must dry. Cover it with plastic so that it won't dry too quickly. After a few days, uncover it. Then wait a few more days. When the pot is completely dry, it is ready to be fired in a special oven called a <u>kiln</u>. After the firing, the pot will keep its shape.

You may want to add color to your pot. In this case, you would put a glaze on the pot and fire it in the kiln a second time.

10 Why is the pot covered with plastic?

So keep moisture in the pot for a while

11 In this story, you can tell that a <u>kiln</u> is a—

Ⓕ cover for the pot.

Ⓖ glaze for the pot.

Ⓗ special oven to bake the pot.

Ⓘ special case to store the pot.

12 The first thing you should do when making a pot is to—

Ⓐ press and squeeze out all the lumps and air bubbles from the clay.

Ⓑ cover the clay with plastic.

Ⓒ shape the clay into a ball.

Ⓓ make the base of the pot.

13 Why should you turn the pot after each squeeze?

Ⓕ so the pot will keep its shape

Ⓖ so the pot will have a base

Ⓗ so the pot won't be too thick in some spots

Ⓘ to remove your thumb

An Invitation

Holiday Fun!

All members of the Boys and Girls Club of Smithtown are invited to a Fourth of July party on July 4, 1998. The party will be held at the home of club sponsors Frank and Marie Brown.

The party will start at 6:30 P.M. Hamburgers, potato salad, watermelon, and other goodies will be served. Bring your turtle for the annual turtle race. At dark, fireworks will be viewed from the balcony. Sparklers and noisemakers will be provided. A marshmallow roast will be held following the fireworks.

It should be a lot of fun. See you on the 4th!

---

14 When will the party take place?

July 4, 1998

15 What should the guests bring?

- Ⓐ a turtle ✓
- Ⓑ watermelon
- Ⓒ a swimsuit
- Ⓓ potato salad

16 According to the invitation, after the fireworks, the guests will—

- Ⓕ eat ice cream.
- Ⓖ race turtles.
- Ⓗ roast marshmallows. ✓
- Ⓙ eat dinner.

17 What time will the party start?

- Ⓐ 6:30 P.M. ✓
- Ⓑ 2:00 P.M.
- Ⓒ 10:00 A.M.
- Ⓓ You cannot tell from the invitation.

GO ON

Learning About Apples

People have been eating apples for a very long time. When the first pioneers came to America, there were only small, sour apples called crab apples. These apples were not good to eat. Later, pioneers brought apple seeds from their homes in Europe.

In 1625 a man in Boston planted the first apple <u>orchard</u> in America. After that, when a pioneer family picked a place to live, one of the first things they did was choose an area and plant apple seeds. Soon, there were many apple trees in America.

The pioneers used apples in many ways. They made apple juice, apple butter, and apple pie. Sometimes they used apples as food for their animals.

Today we have refrigerators and grocery stores. We have fresh fruits and vegetables even in the winter. They are trucked in from warm places and sold in our stores. But the pioneers had no trucks or stores. They had no fresh fruits and vegetables during the long winters.

The pioneers soon learned how to <u>preserve</u> fruits and vegetables. They found that if fruit was dried, it would last and would not spoil. They could make apples last through the winter.

In the fall they picked the apples. Then many families would meet for a work party. They would talk and work at the same time. They peeled the apples and cut out the cores. Then they sliced the apples and laid them on a big net. About a week later, the apples were dried. They would keep for many months. The apples could be eaten dried, or they could be soaked in water and made into pies.

▶GO ON

18 What does the word <u>orchard</u> mean?

   Ⓕ a type of apple

   Ⓖ a pioneer

   Ⓗ a group of fruit trees ✓

   Ⓙ a type of store

19 Why did the pioneers have work parties to dry the apples?

   Ⓐ to make them dry faster ✓

   Ⓑ to visit and work at the same time

   Ⓒ to earn money

   Ⓓ to find new jobs

20 Why were apple seeds brought to America by the pioneers?

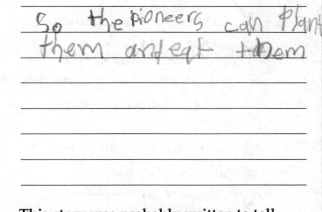

So the pioneers can Plant them and eat them

21 This story was probably written to tell—

   Ⓕ about pioneer work parties.

   Ⓖ about the first apple orchard in America.

   Ⓗ how to preserve apples.

   Ⓙ about the history of the apple in America. ✓

22 If the story continued, it would probably be about—

   Ⓐ other uses for apples. ✓

   Ⓑ how to build a barn.

   Ⓒ the differences between apples and oranges.

   Ⓓ pioneers in New York

23 The pioneers used apples in all the following ways <u>except</u> as—

   Ⓕ food for animals.

   Ⓖ juice.

   Ⓗ butter.

   Ⓙ a glue. ✓

24 You would probably find this story in a book called—

   Ⓐ *A History of America's Favorite Foods.*

   Ⓑ *Orchard Do's and Don'ts.*

   Ⓒ *Famous Early Americans.*

   Ⓓ *How to Preserve Fruits.* ✓

25 In this story, the word <u>preserve</u> means—

   Ⓕ to keep from spoiling. ✓

   Ⓖ to eat quickly.

   Ⓗ to put in a freezer.

   Ⓙ to bury in a trunk in the sand.

26 In order to answer question 25, the reader should—

   Ⓐ look for the word <u>preserve</u> in the story.

   Ⓑ reread the last word in each paragraph.

   Ⓒ read other stories about apples.

   Ⓓ reread the first sentence in each paragraph.

▶ GO ON ▶

A Lifelong Love

When Jane Goodall was a young girl, she liked to watch animals. She learned many things about animals by watching them eat, sleep, and play. When she was older, Jane went to Africa to study wild chimpanzees. She had to live in the jungle to be near the chimpanzees all the time. It was hard for Jane at first. The chimpanzees ran whenever she came near. Soon they were more comfortable when she was around. They let her watch them. She learned how they collected vines and made them into beds in the tops of trees. She found that they greeted each other with noises and hugs. Jane also found that the chimpanzees used tools. They poked grass into the dirt to find bugs to eat.

27 **What tool did the chimpanzees use?**

　Ⓕ　dirt

　Ⓖ　bugs

　Ⓗ　vines

　Ⓙ　grass

28 **Why did the chimpanzees collect vines?**

to make beds

29 **Why did the chimpanzees run from Jane at first?**

　Ⓐ　They were scared of her.

　Ⓑ　They were playing hide-and-seek.

　Ⓒ　They were racing each other.

　Ⓓ　They were looking for food.

30 **This story is mainly about—**

　Ⓕ　wild chimpanzees and how they live.

　Ⓖ　Jane Goodall's study of wild chimpanzees.

　Ⓗ　foods that chimpanzees eat.

　Ⓙ　Jane Goodall's life.

STOP

Test

Sample A **Kangaroos**

Kangaroos come in all sizes. The smallest kangaroo is the musky rat. It is about six inches tall. The largest kangaroo is the red kangaroo. It is about six feet tall. It lives in the dry central part of Australia. Red kangaroos are great jumpers.

How tall is a musky rat?

Ⓐ about six feet

Ⓑ about six centimeters

Ⓒ about six inches

Ⓓ very tiny

Directions: Read each story carefully. Then read each question. Darken the circle for the correct answer, or write in the answer.

The Great Sphinx

The Egyptians made statues of sphinxes to honor kings or queens. A sphinx has the head of a human and the body of a lion. The oldest and largest sphinx is the Great Sphinx. It was built in the desert near Giza, Egypt, thousands of years ago. It is 240 feet long and 66 feet high. At times the Great Sphinx has been buried by sand. Weather has worn away part of the stone. Today scientists are working on ways to save the Great Sphinx. They hope special chemicals will keep it from crumbling.

1 Why was the Great Sphinx built?

Ⓐ to honor a king or queen

Ⓑ to honor lions

Ⓒ to protect Giza, Egypt

Ⓓ to attract tourists

2 How do scientists plan to save the Great Sphinx?

Chemical

▶GO ON

Going to the Store

One day Mrs. Rodriguez was cooking dinner. She called her son Gabriel into the kitchen. "Please ride your bike to the store, and buy a dozen eggs," she said. She gave Gabriel two dollar bills.

On the way to the store, Gabriel passed his friend Eduardo's house. Gabriel stopped to talk for a few minutes. Then he left for the store.

At the store he found the eggs. But when he reached in his pocket, there was no money. The money had fallen out of his pocket. Gabriel got on his bike and <u>retraced</u> his path. He kept his eyes on the street the entire time.

When Gabriel rode up to Eduardo's house, Eduardo came running toward him. "Hey, look what I found!" he said, waving two dollars. "Let's go to the store and buy some ice cream!"

Gabriel grinned. "That's the money I just lost," he said. "I have to buy eggs with it." Eduardo looked disappointed, but he handed the money to Gabriel. "Why don't you ride your bike to the store with me?" Gabriel asked. The two boys raced down the street. They reached the store quickly. Gabriel bought the eggs. But he had forgotten to bring his backpack for carrying them. He decided the safest thing to do was to zip the eggs inside his jacket.

He had just zipped his jacket when Eduardo called out, "Race you to the corner!" Gabriel stood up to get extra speed. But his jacket was not tight enough to hold the eggs. The carton crashed to the street. Gabriel stopped and opened it. "Wow, I sure hope Mom doesn't need more than three eggs," he said to himself.

3 **What is this story mainly about?**

   Ⓕ what happened to Eduardo after school

   Ⓖ what Mrs. Rodriguez prepared for dinner

   Ⓗ what Gabriel ate for supper

   ● what happened when Gabriel went shopping

4 **What will probably happen next?**

   Ⓐ Mrs. Rodriguez will be happy to see Gabriel.

   Ⓑ Mrs. Rodriguez will reward Gabriel.

   ● Mrs. Rodriguez will be unhappy with Gabriel.

   Ⓓ Eduardo will return to the store.

5 **How many eggs were left unbroken?**

   Ⓕ none

   ● three

   Ⓗ five

   Ⓙ ten

6 **What did Eduardo want to do with the two dollars?**

   ● buy ice cream

   Ⓑ save it

   Ⓒ give it away

   Ⓓ buy a game

7 **Mrs. Rodriguez sent Gabriel to the store—**

   Ⓕ to return empty pop bottles.

   Ⓖ to pay a bill.

   Ⓗ to buy eggs.

   Ⓙ to meet his father.

8 **What caused the eggs to break?**

   The Jacket

9 **Eduardo rode to the store with Gabriel—**

   ● after dinner.

   Ⓑ the second time Gabriel went to the store.

   Ⓒ after lunch.

   Ⓓ the first time Gabriel went to the store.

10 **In this story, the word retraced means—**

   ● went back over the same path.

   Ⓖ cooked again.

   Ⓗ jumped again.

   Ⓙ laughed again.

▶GO ON▶

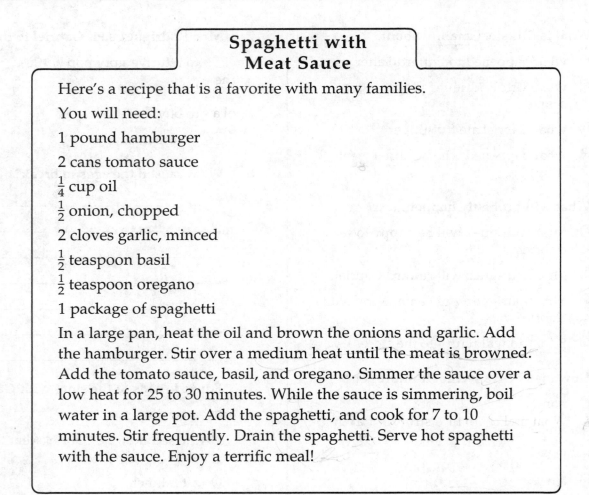

Spaghetti with Meat Sauce

Here's a recipe that is a favorite with many families.

You will need:

1 pound hamburger

2 cans tomato sauce

$\frac{1}{4}$ cup oil

$\frac{1}{2}$ onion, chopped

2 cloves garlic, minced

$\frac{1}{2}$ teaspoon basil

$\frac{1}{2}$ teaspoon oregano

1 package of spaghetti

In a large pan, heat the oil and brown the onions and garlic. Add the hamburger. Stir over a medium heat until the meat is browned. Add the tomato sauce, basil, and oregano. Simmer the sauce over a low heat for 25 to 30 minutes. While the sauce is simmering, boil water in a large pot. Add the spaghetti, and cook for 7 to 10 minutes. Stir frequently. Drain the spaghetti. Serve hot spaghetti with the sauce. Enjoy a terrific meal!

11 **How should you prepare the onion for cooking?**

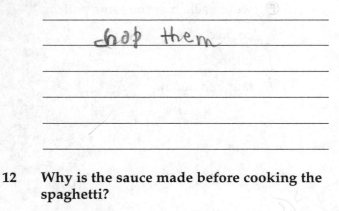

chop them

12 **Why is the sauce made before cooking the spaghetti?**

Ⓐ The sauce is served first.

Ⓑ The sauce needs time to cook.

Ⓒ It takes more time to cook the spaghetti.

Ⓓ Most people like the sauce better.

13 **When making spaghetti with meat sauce, the first step is to—**

Ⓕ boil water.

Ⓖ cook the hamburger.

Ⓗ add the tomato sauce.

Ⓙ heat the oil.

14 **This recipe tells you to do all the following except—**

Ⓐ add basil and oregano.

Ⓑ add sliced mushrooms.

Ⓒ add chopped onions.

Ⓓ add two cans of tomato sauce.

GO ON

A Great Woman

Mae C. Jemison grew up in Chicago, Illinois. Even as a young girl she dreamed of one day becoming an astronaut. She worked hard in school and earned excellent grades.

Mae's extraordinary efforts in grade school and high school gave her the opportunity to go to Stanford University in California. It was there that she received a degree in engineering. Next, Mae enrolled in Cornell University Medical College in New York City. She received a medical degree at this college.

Her dream of becoming an astronaut came true in 1987, when she was accepted in the astronaut program. In 1992, when Jemison was 35 years old, she became the first African-American female astronaut to go into space. She was aboard the space shuttle *Endeavour* along with six other astronauts. The mission of the crew members of the *Endeavour* was to test the effects of weightlessness on certain animals such as frogs and fish.

15 **What question does the last paragraph answer?**

(F) How does weightlessness affect certain animals?

(G) What makes up the astronaut training program?

(H) How did Mae C. Jemison's dream come true?

(J) Where is Stanford University?

16 **What was the mission of the space shuttle *Endeavour*?**

(A) to take pictures of Earth from space

(B) to test the effect of weightlessness on animals

(C) to launch a satellite into space

(D) to orbit Earth longer than anyone had ever done before

17 **What was Mae C. Jemison's lifelong dream?**

Being an astronot

18 **The author probably wrote this story—**

(F) to describe the mission of the space shuttle *Endeavour*.

(G) to describe the career of Mae C. Jemison.

(H) to describe the childhood of Mae C. Jemison.

(J) to explain the astronaut-training program.

Helping Each Other

Once an ant was crawling lazily down a country path. As the path curved near a stream, the ant realized he was thirsty. The rushing water looked so cool and clear that the ant could hardly wait to take a sip. Suddenly a gust of wind blew the poor ant right into the stream.

"Help! Someone, help! I cannot swim!" he yelled.

Up in a tree not far away, a dove heard the ant's cry for help. She reached up and with her bill plucked a small branch off the tree. In a flash she flew down to where the ant was struggling to stay above water. Carefully she lowered the branch to the water's surface near the ant.

"If you can climb onto the branch, I will carry you to safety," cooed the dove.

The ant gratefully climbed onto the branch. Then the dove lifted the branch from the water and placed it safely on the grassy bank. The ant shook water from his eyes, took a few deep breaths, and looked around to thank the dove. But the dove had flown to the top of a nearby tree.

With a wave of thanks toward the dove, the ant started back down the path. He had only gone a short distance when he noticed a hunter aiming a rifle at the helpful dove.

"This will not do!" exclaimed the ant. He hurried as fast as he could toward the hunter. The angry ant climbed with great purpose over the hunter's large brown shoe and made his way under the hunter's pants leg. Just in the nick of time, the ant took a healthy bite from the hunter's ankle. The hunter let out a loud howl of pain. The noise startled the dove, and she flew from her treetop perch to safety.

GO ON

19 **What did the dove use to save the ant?**

(A) a boat

(B) a branch

(C) her wing

(D) a leaf

20 **What caused the dove to fly to safety?**

(F) a rifle shot

(G) the ant's scream

(H) the hunter's howl

(J) a snapping branch

21 **According to the story, the ant got a drink of water from a—**

(A) puddle of water in the road.

(B) drop of rain on a leaf.

(C) leaf.

(D) stream.

22 **Who heard the ant's cry for help?**

(F) a dove

(G) the hunter

(H) a fish

(J) a butterfly

23 **What most likely would have happened if the ant had not bitten the hunter?**

(A) The hunter would have stepped on the ant.

(B) The dove would have been shot.

(C) The hunter would have fallen into the stream.

(D) The dove would have gone with the ant.

24 **Why did the ant fall into the water?**

Because of the big wind

25 **You can tell this story is make-believe because—**

(F) it has a hunter in it.

(G) animals talk in it.

(H) an ant climbs onto a branch.

(J) a dove flies to a treetop.

26 **What lesson can be learned from this story?**

(A) Don't bite the hand that feeds you.

(B) A stitch in time saves nine.

(C) Slow and steady wins the race.

(D) One good turn deserves another.

27 **This story was probably written to—**

(F) teach the reader about ants.

(G) show how ants can survive in water.

(H) discourage people from hunting.

(J) teach a lesson about helping others.

28 **You would most likely find this story in a book called—**

(A) *Country Days.*

(B) *Real-Life Animal Friends.*

(C) *Learning from Animal Tales.*

(D) *How to Hunt.*

STOP

UNIT FOUR
Reading Vocabulary

Understanding Word Meanings

Directions: Darken the circle for the word or words that have the <u>same</u> or <u>almost the same</u> meaning as the underlined word, or write in the answer.

Sample A

A <u>check</u> is a kind of—

Ⓐ box

Ⓑ picture

Ⓒ dance

Ⓓ mark

STOP

1 **<u>Slender</u> means—**

Ⓐ quick

Ⓑ shy

Ⓒ thin

Ⓓ lost

2 **What is an <u>ache</u>?**

Pain

3 **A <u>cap</u> is a kind of—**

Ⓕ lock

Ⓖ hat

Ⓗ head

Ⓙ coat

4 **To <u>connect</u> is to—**

Ⓐ hit

Ⓑ shut

Ⓒ join

Ⓓ belong

5 **<u>Savage</u> means—**

Ⓕ hungry

Ⓖ wild

Ⓗ comfortable

Ⓙ large

6 **To <u>oppose</u> something is to—**

Ⓐ cheer for it

Ⓑ be against it

Ⓒ leave it

Ⓓ want it

STOP

Matching Words with More Than One Meaning

Directions: Darken the circle for the sentence in which the underlined word means the same as it does in the sentence in the box.

| TRY THIS | Read the sentence in the box carefully. Decide what the underlined word means. Then look for the sentence in which the underlined word has the same meaning. |

Sample A

> A <u>wave</u> swept over the beach.

In which sentence does <u>wave</u> have the same meaning as it does in the sentence above?

Ⓐ We saw the flag <u>wave</u> in the wind.

Ⓑ Her hair has a natural <u>wave</u>.

Ⓒ I saw the pilot <u>wave</u> to me.

Ⓓ The fish jumped above the <u>wave</u>.

| THINK IT THROUGH | The correct answer is <u>D</u>. In the sentence, The fish jumped above the wave, <u>wave</u> means the same as it does in the sentence in the box. A wave is "a wall of water." |

 STOP

1

> She wore a <u>circle</u> of flowers in her hair.

In which sentence does <u>circle</u> have the same meaning as it does in the sentence above?

Ⓐ The plane will <u>circle</u> the field.

Ⓑ Draw a <u>circle</u> on the paper.

Ⓒ Cara belongs to a sewing <u>circle</u>.

Ⓓ <u>Circle</u> your answers.

2

> Let's go out and <u>play</u>.

In which sentence does <u>play</u> have the same meaning as it does in the sentence above?

Ⓕ The band will <u>play</u> a new song.

Ⓖ My team will <u>play</u> our first game today.

Ⓗ My sister wrote a <u>play</u>.

Ⓙ Please come to my house to <u>play</u>.

3

> That boy lives on our <u>block</u>.

In which sentence does <u>block</u> have the same meaning as it does in the sentence above?

Ⓐ Use this board to <u>block</u> the hole.

Ⓑ The baby dropped the toy <u>block</u>.

Ⓒ We drove around the <u>block</u>.

Ⓓ She carved that <u>block</u> of marble.

4

> May I borrow some <u>string</u>?

In which sentence does <u>string</u> have the same meaning as it does in the sentence above?

Ⓕ He helped me <u>string</u> the lights.

Ⓖ I bought a <u>string</u> of pearls.

Ⓗ Cut the <u>string</u> on this package.

Ⓙ My guitar <u>string</u> is broken.

 STOP

Using Context Clues

Directions: Darken the circle for the word or words that give the meaning of the underlined word, or write in the answer.

Sample A

A family finally moved into the house that has been <u>vacant</u> for six months. <u>Vacant</u> means—

Ⓐ white

Ⓑ empty

Ⓒ burned

Ⓓ built

STOP

---

1 You should not play with matches because you might <u>harm</u> yourself. <u>Harm</u> means—

Ⓐ hurt

Ⓑ help

Ⓒ calm

Ⓓ see

2 Instead of eating french fries, I ate something <u>beneficial</u> to my health. <u>Beneficial</u> means—

Ⓕ damaging

Ⓖ helpful

Ⓗ equal

Ⓙ thankful

3 The wagon train couldn't go around the river, so they had to <u>ford</u> it. <u>Ford</u> means—

Ⓐ drain

Ⓑ paddle

Ⓒ fish

Ⓓ cross

4 To <u>observe</u> hamsters at play, you must see them at night. <u>Observe</u> means—

Ⓕ watch

Ⓖ hear

Ⓗ control

Ⓙ do

5 We need a new song for our play, so our teacher will <u>compose</u> one. <u>Compose</u> means—

Ⓐ sell

Ⓑ hum

Ⓒ write

Ⓓ use

6 The <u>instructions</u> on the label say that you should wash that shirt in cold water. What are <u>instructions</u>?

directions

STOP

Test

Sample A

A <u>nursery</u> is a place for—

- (A) machines
- (B) sleds
- (C) nests
- (D) babies ●

🛑STOP

For questions 1–9, darken the circle for the word or words that have the same or almost the same meaning as the underlined word, or write in the answer.

1 <u>Simple</u> means—

- (A) smart
- (B) cheap
- (C) late
- (D) easy ●

2 To <u>trade</u> something is to—

- (F) exchange it ●
- (G) collect it
- (H) leave it
- (J) keep it

3 A <u>kettle</u> is a kind of—

- (A) food
- (B) pot ●
- (C) chair
- (D) basket

4 A <u>policy</u> is a kind of—

- (F) plan ●
- (G) sea bird
- (H) hood
- (J) envelope

5 Something that is <u>accepted</u> is—

- (A) received ●
- (B) stolen
- (C) pretty
- (D) wrapped

6 A <u>meadow</u> is most like a—

- (F) vase
- (G) garden ●
- (H) store
- (J) field

7 A <u>yacht</u> is a kind of—

- (A) deer ●
- (B) boat
- (C) hat
- (D) pickle

8 To <u>tremble</u> means to—

- (F) wave
- (G) laugh
- (H) cough
- (J) shake ●

9 What does it mean to <u>slice</u> something?

cut something

🛑STOP

Sample B

> My picture hangs <u>above</u> the fireplace.

In which sentence does <u>above</u> have the same meaning as it does in the sentence in the box?

- Ⓐ I had to shout <u>above</u> the noise.
- Ⓑ The huge flock of birds filled the skies <u>above</u>.
- Ⓒ Your book is on the shelf <u>above</u> the desk.
- Ⓓ His scores are <u>above</u> average.

For questions 10–14, darken the circle for the sentence in which the underlined word means the same as it does in the sentence in the box.

10

> The rule was <u>fair</u> to both teams.

In which sentence does <u>fair</u> have the same meaning as it does in the sentence above?

- Ⓐ Let's go to the state <u>fair</u>.
- Ⓑ Our teacher told us to play <u>fair</u>.
- Ⓒ The weather today was <u>fair</u>.
- Ⓓ She has very <u>fair</u> hair.

11

> We found Grandfather's old sailor's <u>chest</u> in the attic.

In which sentence does <u>chest</u> have the same meaning as it does in the sentence above?

- Ⓕ My brother caught a <u>chest</u> cold.
- Ⓖ My shirts are in the third drawer of my <u>chest</u>.
- Ⓗ The pirates put their treasure in a <u>chest</u>.
- Ⓙ The football hit him in the <u>chest</u>.

12

> Al will <u>act</u> the hero's part.

In which sentence does <u>act</u> have the same meaning as it does in the sentence above?

- Ⓐ I would love to <u>act</u> in a movie.
- Ⓑ We liked the third <u>act</u> of the play.
- Ⓒ She told us to <u>act</u> like gentlemen.
- Ⓓ The soldier performed a brave <u>act</u>.

13

> Draw a picture in this <u>space</u>.

In which sentence does <u>space</u> have the same meaning as it does in the sentence above?

- Ⓕ It came from outer <u>space</u>.
- Ⓖ <u>Space</u> the letters evenly on the line.
- Ⓗ A <u>space</u> of two weeks followed.
- Ⓙ Leave a <u>space</u> for your name.

14

> What <u>time</u> does the show start?

In which sentence does <u>time</u> have the same meaning as it does in the sentence above?

- Ⓐ The coach will <u>time</u> my race.
- Ⓑ I had a good <u>time</u> at the party.
- Ⓒ Try to keep <u>time</u> with the music.
- Ⓓ It is now <u>time</u> to return to class.

Sample C

The <u>unsafe</u> trail was marked with a warning sign. <u>Unsafe</u> means—

- Ⓐ scenic
- Ⓑ hilly
- Ⓒ dangerous
- Ⓓ winding

For questions 15–21, darken the circle for the word or words that give the meaning of the underlined word, or write in the answer.

15 Instead of dull gray, I wanted to paint my room <u>vivid</u> yellow. <u>Vivid</u> means—

- Ⓕ bright
- Ⓖ dark
- Ⓗ lemon
- Ⓙ cool

16 If you don't want to buy a boat, you can <u>charter</u> one for your fishing trip. <u>Charter</u> means—

- Ⓐ choose
- Ⓑ sail
- Ⓒ rent
- Ⓓ trade

17 We like everything in the show, but our favorite <u>segment</u> is the pet tricks. <u>Segment</u> means—

- Ⓕ actor
- Ⓖ song
- Ⓗ part
- Ⓙ star

18 We tried to open the trunk, but the lid would not <u>budge</u>. <u>Budge</u> means—

- Ⓐ slam
- Ⓑ rest
- Ⓒ move
- Ⓓ burn

19 Wild horses <u>roam</u> freely in Nevada. <u>Roam</u> means—

- Ⓕ sleep
- Ⓖ wander
- Ⓗ eat
- Ⓙ hide

20 Because I was tired, I <u>neglected</u> to do my exercises. <u>Neglected</u> means—

- Ⓐ tried
- Ⓑ failed
- Ⓒ knew
- Ⓓ meant

21 Our kite was broken, but Uncle Victor helped us <u>repair</u> it. <u>Repair</u> means—

_____

_____

_____

_____

_____

_____

_____

STOP

Math: Problem-Solving Strategies

Overview

The Problem-Solving Plan

When solving math problems follow these steps:

STEP 1: WHAT IS THE QUESTION/GOAL?

Decide what must be found. This information is usually presented in the form of a question.

STEP 2: FIND THE FACTS

Locate the factual information in three different ways:

A. KEY FACTS...the facts you need to solve the problem.

B. FACTS YOU DON'T NEED...those facts which are not necessary for solving the problem.

C. ARE MORE FACTS NEEDED?...decide if you have enough information to solve the problem.

STEP 3: SELECT A STRATEGY

Decide what you can do to solve the problem.

STEP 4: SOLVE

Use your plan to solve the problem.

STEP 5: DOES YOUR RESPONSE MAKE SENSE?

Think about your answer. Does it make sense?

PROBLEM/QUESTION:

Jackie is going shopping for presents in Green's Toy Store. Mr. Green sells toy bears for $1.98, toy dogs for $1.50, toy cats for $1.45, toy birds for $1.10 and toy snakes for $.88. She can buy only one of each toy animal. Jackie has $5.00 to spend. What is the greatest number of toys she can buy?

STEP 1: WHAT IS THE QUESTION/GOAL?

STEP 2: FIND THE FACTS

STEP 3: SELECT A STRATEGY

STEP 4: SOLVE

STEP 5: DOES YOUR RESPONSE MAKE SENSE?

Problem 2

PROBLEM/QUESTION:

Eduardo has a choice of 4 possible outfits that he can wear today. He has one striped and one solid shirt. He also has a pair of black pants and a pair of blue pants. Describe the 4 combinations of shirts and pants Eduardo can make.

STEP 1: WHAT IS THE QUESTION/GOAL?

STEP 2: FIND THE FACTS

STEP 3: SELECT A STRATEGY

STEP 4: SOLVE

STEP 5: DOES YOUR RESPONSE MAKE SENSE?

Understanding Numeration

Directions: Darken the circle for the correct answer, or write in the answer.

> **TRY THIS**
>
> Read each problem carefully. Be sure to think about which numbers stand for hundreds, tens, and ones.

Sample A

Which is another way to write 238?

Ⓐ 20 + 380

Ⓑ 200 + 30 + 8

Ⓒ 200 + 30 + 80

Ⓓ 2,000 + 30 + 8

> **THINK IT THROUGH**
>
> The correct answer is <u>B</u>. 200 + 30 + 8 = 238. Therefore, 238 = <u>200 + 30 + 8</u>.

🛑 STOP

1 Juanita baked an odd number of muffins to take to the bake sale. How many muffins did she bake?

Ⓐ 17 muffins

Ⓑ 16 muffins

Ⓒ 12 muffins

Ⓓ 10 muffins

2

Name	Points
Chris	192
Fatima	150
Mike	269
Gwen	148

Which child scored the most number of points in a computer game?

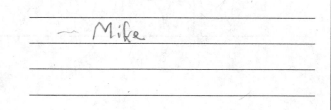

Mike

3 Which number belongs in the box on the number line?

```
←——|———|———|———|———|——→
   40  45  ☐      60
```

46	50	55	58
Ⓕ	Ⓖ	Ⓗ	Ⓙ

4 The chart shows how long it takes to grow 4 kinds of plants.

Corn	Beans	Tomatoes	Peppers
72 days	43 days	60 days	54 days

Which group shows these plants listed in order from shortest to longest growing time?

Ⓐ beans, peppers, tomatoes, corn

Ⓑ peppers, beans, tomatoes, corn

Ⓒ corn, beans, tomatoes, peppers

Ⓓ tomatoes, peppers, beans, corn

🛑 STOP

Using Whole Numbers, Fractions, and Decimals

Directions: Darken the circle for the correct answer, or write in the answer.

Sample A

What is another way to write 4 + 4 + 4 ?

Ⓐ 3 + 4

Ⓑ 3 × 4

Ⓒ 4 × 4 × 4

Ⓓ 12 + 4

THINK IT THROUGH The correct answer is **B, 3 × 4**. 4 + 4 + 4 = 12. Choice B, 3 × 4, is the only answer that equals 12.

---

1 What fraction of the shape is not shaded?

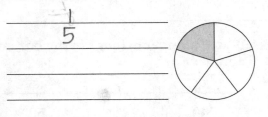

2

Name	Number of Inches
Yoshi	1.9
Penelope	2.1
Marcus	1.7
Felicia	2.4

Which child grew the most inches in a year?

Ⓐ Yoshi

Ⓑ Penelope

Ⓒ Marcus

Ⓓ Felicia

3 Which number belongs in the box to make the number sentence correct?

$$7 \times \square = 7$$

7   6   1   0

Ⓕ   Ⓖ   Ⓗ   Ⓙ

4 Which number sentence is in the same fact family as

$$8 + 3 = 11 \quad ?$$

Ⓐ 8 × 3 = 24

Ⓑ 5 + 6 = 11

Ⓒ 11 − 3 = 8

Ⓓ 11 + 3 = 14

5 Which group of balloons has $\frac{1}{3}$ of the balloons shaded?

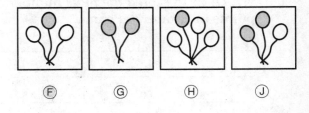

Ⓕ   Ⓖ   Ⓗ   Ⓙ

58

Understanding Patterns and Relationships

Directions: Darken the circle for the correct answer, or write in the answer.

Read each question carefully. Look at each answer choice to see which number or figure will answer the question correctly.

Sample A

What missing number completes the pattern in the boxes?

46	42	38	34	

THINK IT THROUGH

The correct answer is <u>A</u>, <u>30</u>. The numbers in the pattern decrease by 4. So, the correct answer is 30, because 34 − 4 = 30.

- Ⓐ 30
- Ⓑ 32
- Ⓒ 33
- Ⓓ 35

STOP

---

1 Which of these shows the missing piece of the figure?

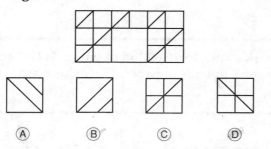

- Ⓐ
- Ⓑ
- Ⓒ
- Ⓓ

2 Which of these shows the missing piece of the figure?

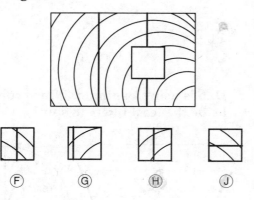

- Ⓕ
- Ⓖ
- Ⓗ
- Ⓙ

3 What missing number completes the pattern in the boxes?

73	75	77		81

- Ⓐ 77
- Ⓑ 78
- Ⓒ 79
- Ⓓ 80

4 Each juice carton holds 6 drinks. What missing number completes the pattern in the chart?

Number of Drinks	
Number of Cartons of Grape Juice	Number of Drinks
2	12
3	18
4	?
5	30

_____

_____

_____

_____

STOP

Working with Statistics and Probability

Directions: Darken the circle for the correct answer, or write in the answer.

TRY THIS Look at each chart, graph, or picture. Then read the question carefully. Look for words or numbers in the question that tell you what information to find.

Sample A

The tally chart shows the number of pounds of litter Kyle collected on a cleanup project.

How many pounds of paper did Kyle collect?

Ⓐ 2

Ⓑ 7

Ⓒ 8

Ⓓ 10

Litter Collected

Paper	卌 卌
Metal	卌
Plastic	卌 ||
Cloth	||
Other	卌 |

THINK IT THROUGH The correct answer is <u>D</u>, <u>10</u>. Each tally mark stands for 1 pound of paper. Each group of 4 tally marks with a slash stands for 5 pounds of paper. Since there are 2 groups, 5 + 5 = 10 pounds of paper.

STOP

The graph below shows the pets owned by students in Mr. Ito's class. Study the graph and answer questions 1 and 2.

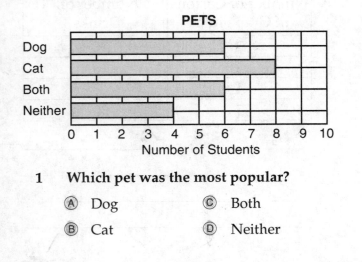

PETS

Dog, Cat, Both, Neither

Number of Students

1 Which pet was the most popular?

Ⓐ Dog   Ⓒ Both

Ⓑ Cat   Ⓓ Neither

2 How many more students owned cats than dogs?

Ⓕ 2   Ⓗ 5

Ⓖ 3   Ⓙ 6

3 Dan is using a spinner. Which color will he be the least likely to spin?

_____ Yellow

_____

_____

_____

_____

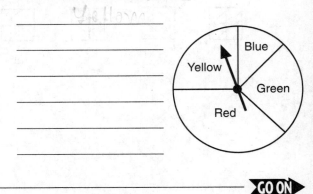

GO ON

60

4 The students in Ms. Iannatti's class made this chart to count the fruit they ate in one day.

Fruit	Number Eaten
Bananas	8
Plums	2
Oranges	12
Apples	16
Peaches	4

Which kind of fruit did students eat exactly 2 times as many of as bananas?

Ⓐ Peaches

Ⓑ Bananas

Ⓒ Oranges

Ⓓ Apples

5 The tally chart shows the favorite subjects of the students in Mrs. Fine's class.

Favorite Subject for Third-Grade Students

Science	|||
Social Studies	ⵀ| l
Math	ⵀ| ||||
Language	ⵀ| |||

How many students liked language?

Ⓕ 3

Ⓖ 6

Ⓗ 8

Ⓙ 9

6 Look at the cards shown here.

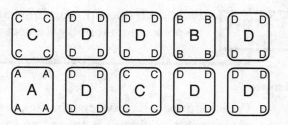

If Kevin picks a card without looking, which will he most likely choose?

Ⓐ A   Ⓒ C

Ⓑ B   Ⓓ D

7 Ellen collected these shells in a bucket.

	3
	12
	2
	4

If she picks 1 shell out of the bucket without looking, which kind will it most likely be?

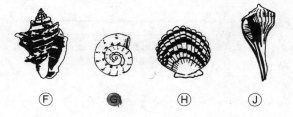

Ⓕ   Ⓖ   Ⓗ   Ⓙ

STOP

Understanding Geometry

Directions: Darken the circle for the correct answer, or write in the answer.

Sample A

Which figure will have two halves that match exactly when it is folded on the solid line?

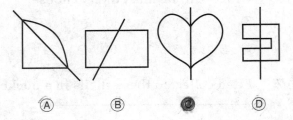

Ⓐ   Ⓑ   Ⓒ   Ⓓ

🛑 STOP

---

1 Everyone at Shari's birthday party wore a party hat like the one shown here. What shape does the hat have?

- Ⓐ cone
- Ⓑ pyramid
- Ⓒ cube
- Ⓓ sphere

2 Look at the numbered shapes. Which two are exactly the same in size and shape?

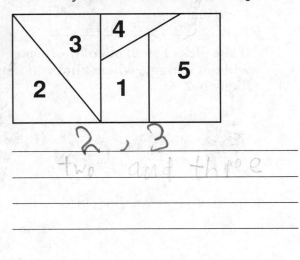

2, 3
two and three

3 Which shape has four corners and four sides exactly the same size?

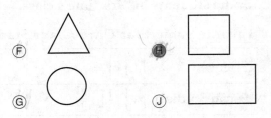

Ⓕ   Ⓗ   Ⓖ   Ⓙ

4 Moira drew this figure on her paper.

1

What did it look like when she turned it upside down?

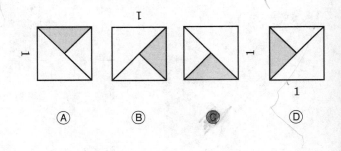

Ⓐ   Ⓑ   Ⓒ   Ⓓ

🛑 STOP

Working with Measurement

Directions: Darken the circle for the correct answer, or write in the answer.

TRY THIS	Look at each picture or object shown. Then read the question carefully. Look for words or numbers in the question that tell you what information to find.

Sample A

Cliff ate lunch at 12:00 noon. He went to the park one and one-half hours later. Which clock shows the time Cliff went to the park?

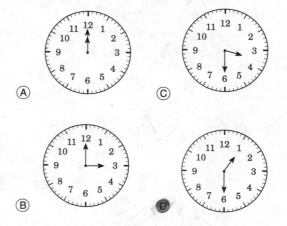

Ⓐ   Ⓒ

Ⓑ   Ⓓ

THINK IT THROUGH	The correct answer is D, 1:30 P.M. If Cliff ate lunch at 12:00 noon, an hour and one-half hour later is 1:30 P.M.

STOP

---

1 Use your centimeter ruler to help answer this question.

How many centimeters long is the toy bus?

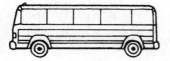
4 cm

2 Which unit of measurement is best to use to describe the amount of juice in a jar?

Ⓐ cups   Ⓒ pounds

Ⓑ inches   Ⓓ teaspoons

3 Monica found a dime, a nickel, and a quarter in her coat pocket.

What is the value of the money shown?

Ⓕ 45¢   Ⓗ 36¢

Ⓖ 40¢   Ⓙ 31¢

GO ON

4   Marc bought a package of drawing paper that cost 59¢. He gave the clerk 75¢. How much change should Marc get back?

Ⓐ

Ⓑ

Ⓒ

Ⓓ

5   Jennifer is going to shovel snow off the sidewalk. What is the temperature like outside?

Ⓕ   92°

Ⓖ   75°

Ⓗ   51°

Ⓙ   30°

6   Mrs. Traub feeds the animals who live behind her house. Which animal lives the shortest distance from Mrs. Traub's house?

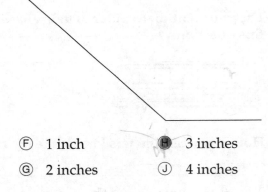

Ⓐ   Ⓑ   Ⓒ   Ⓓ

7   Terrell drew 2 lines. Use your inch ruler to measure the total length of the lines.

Ⓕ   1 inch   Ⓗ   3 inches

Ⓖ   2 inches   Ⓙ   4 inches

Solving Problems

Directions: Darken the circle for the correct answer, or write in the answer.

> **TRY THIS** Study the words in each problem carefully. Then decide what you have to do to find the answer.

Sample A

Igor blew up 4 fewer balloons than Andy. Andy blew up 6 balloons more than Betsy. Betsy blew up 10 balloons. How many balloons did Igor blow up?

Ⓐ 20

Ⓑ 16

Ⓒ 12

Ⓓ 8

THINK IT THROUGH The correct answer is <u>C</u>, <u>12</u>. Betsy blew up 10 balloons. If Andy blew up 6 more than Betsy, he blew up 16 (10 + 6). If Igor blew up 4 fewer than Andy, he blew up 12, since 16 − 4 = 12.

STOP

---

1 Michelle caught 9 fish. She put all of the small fish back into the water. What do you need to know to find out how many fish Michelle took home?

How many small fish are there?

2 There are 4 tour vans at the restaurant. The 32 people on the tour stopped to eat dinner. Which is the most reasonable answer for how many people rode in each van?

Ⓐ 128

Ⓑ 36

Ⓒ 28

Ⓓ 8

3 Marvin collected 45 cans for recycling. Ira collected 39 cans. Which number sentence shows how to find the number of cans they collected altogether?

Ⓕ 39 + n = 45

Ⓖ 45 − 39 = n

Ⓗ 45 − n = 39

Ⓙ 45 + 39 = n

4 What number is inside the triangle, inside the square, and is an odd number?

Ⓐ 2

Ⓑ 5

Ⓒ 7

Ⓓ 9

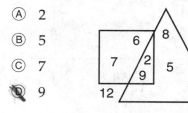

STOP

Math Procedures
Understanding Computation

Directions: Darken the circle for the correct answer. If the correct answer is not given, darken the circle for *NH* for *Not Here*.

Study each problem carefully. Look at the sign to know if you should add, subtract, multiply, or divide. Then work the problem on scratch paper. Be sure to line up the digits. Remember to regroup where necessary.

Sample A

$$15 - \square = 8$$

23	10	8	7	NH
Ⓐ	Ⓑ	Ⓒ	Ⓧ	Ⓔ

STOP

---

1 6)48

8	7	6	5	NH
Ⓐ	Ⓑ	Ⓒ	Ⓓ	Ⓔ

---

2 $9 \div 3 = \square$

6	5	4	3	NH
Ⓕ	Ⓖ	Ⓗ	Ⓙ	Ⓚ

3
$$\begin{array}{r} 22 \\ + 21 \\ \hline \end{array}$$

42	41	39	24	NH
Ⓐ	Ⓑ	Ⓒ	Ⓓ	Ⓔ

4
$$\begin{array}{r} 30 \\ 184 \\ + 76 \\ \hline \end{array}$$

115	124	290	560	NH
Ⓕ	Ⓖ	Ⓗ	Ⓙ	Ⓚ

5
$$\begin{array}{r} 6 \\ \times 3 \\ \hline \end{array}$$

24	18	12	9	NH
Ⓐ	Ⓑ	Ⓒ	Ⓓ	Ⓔ

6
$$\begin{array}{r} 92 \\ - 57 \\ \hline \end{array}$$

35	39	45	149	NH
Ⓕ	Ⓖ	Ⓗ	Ⓙ	Ⓚ

7
$$\begin{array}{r} 549 \\ + 81 \\ \hline \end{array}$$

620	630	720	730	NH
Ⓐ	Ⓑ	Ⓒ	Ⓓ	Ⓔ

8
$$\begin{array}{r} 403 \\ \times 3 \\ \hline \end{array}$$

1,206	1,248	3,208	3,248	NH
Ⓕ	Ⓖ	Ⓗ	Ⓙ	Ⓚ

STOP

Using Computation

Directions: Darken the circle for the correct answer. If the correct answer is not given, darken the circle for *NH* for *Not Here*. If no choices are given, write in the answer.

TRY THIS	Read each problem carefully. Think about what the question is asking. Think about which numbers stand for ones, tens, and hundreds. Work the problem on scratch paper. Regroup where necessary.

Sample A

Tracey is reading a book that has 464 pages. She has read 379 pages. How many pages does she have left to read?

Ⓐ 80

Ⓑ 85

Ⓒ 90

Ⓓ 95

Ⓔ NH

THINK IT THROUGH	The correct answer is <u>B</u>, <u>85</u>. The words "pages left to read" means to subtract 379 from 464 to get <u>85</u>.

STOP

---

1 Eric played a computer game for 17 minutes. He played another game for 14 minutes. How many minutes did Eric play the games altogether?

3	21	31	41	NH
Ⓐ	Ⓑ	Ⓒ	Ⓓ	Ⓔ

2 Perry bought 3 boxes of crayons. There were 6 crayons in each box.

How many crayons did Perry buy altogether?

6+3=9

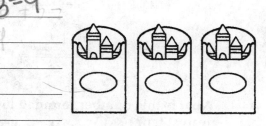

3 On Saturday, 364 children went to the park to celebrate Earth Day.

What is 364 rounded to the nearest hundred?

Ⓕ 300

Ⓖ 350

Ⓗ 360

Ⓙ 400

Ⓚ NH

4 Mrs. Martin had a pizza party for her class. She wrote down the order for the pizzas.

Cheese	Pepperoni	Vegetable
8	5	2

How many pizzas did she buy altogether?

16	15	14	13	NH
Ⓐ	Ⓑ	Ⓒ	Ⓓ	Ⓔ

STOP

Test 1: Math Procedures

Sample A

$$51 \times 2$$

52	53	72	102	NH
Ⓐ	Ⓑ	Ⓒ	Ⓓ	Ⓔ

🛑 STOP

Sample B

Jagdesh bought 12 blue balloons and 14 red balloons. How many balloons did she buy in all?

28	26	22	2	NH
Ⓕ	Ⓖ	Ⓗ	Ⓙ	Ⓚ

🛑 STOP

For questions 1–14, darken the circle for the correct answer. If the correct answer is not here, darken the circle for *NH*. If no choices are given, write in the answer.

1 $32 \div 8 = \square$

5	4	3	2	NH
Ⓐ	Ⓑ	Ⓒ	Ⓓ	Ⓔ

2 $4 \times 21 = \square$

25	62	80	84	NH
Ⓕ	Ⓖ	Ⓗ	Ⓙ	Ⓚ

3 $6 \times 5 = \square$

11	24	30	36	NH
Ⓐ	Ⓑ	Ⓒ	Ⓓ	Ⓔ

4

$$315 + 23$$

328	338	518	545	NH
Ⓕ	Ⓖ	Ⓗ	Ⓙ	Ⓚ

5

$$200 - 164$$

36	46	136	146	NH
Ⓐ	Ⓑ	Ⓒ	Ⓓ	Ⓔ

6

$$460 \times 3$$

790	1,180	1,380	1,383	NH
Ⓕ	Ⓖ	Ⓗ	Ⓙ	Ⓚ

7 $9\overline{)72}$

_____

_____

8   There were 43 pictures sent to an art contest.

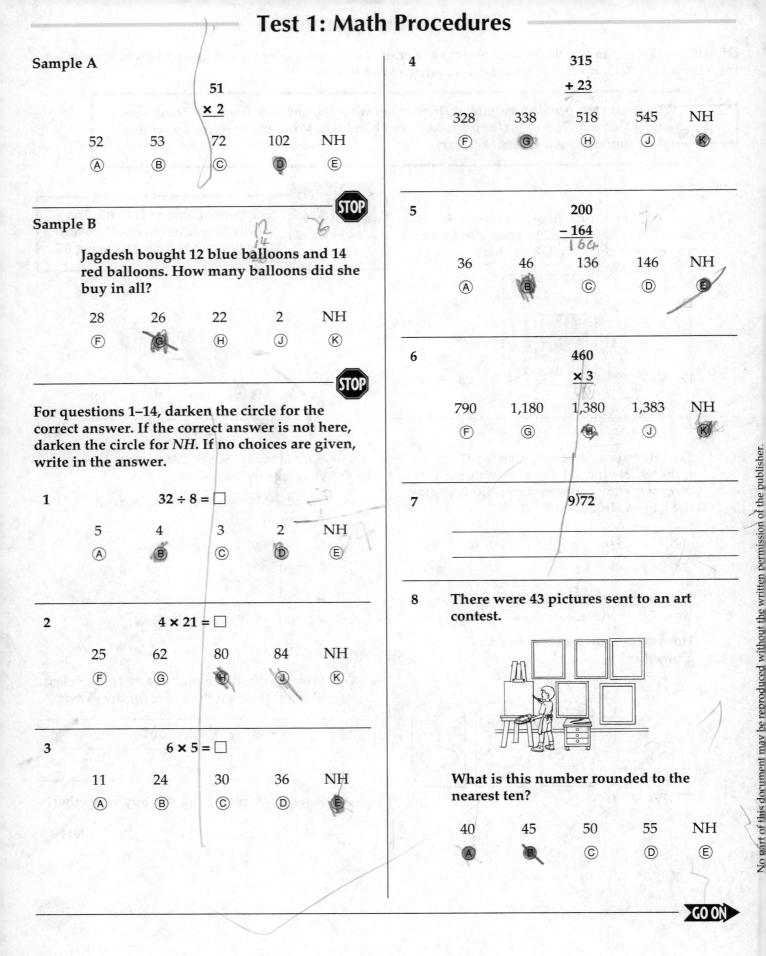

What is this number rounded to the nearest ten?

40	45	50	55	NH
Ⓐ	Ⓑ	Ⓒ	Ⓓ	Ⓔ

▶ GO ON

9 At Talfourd Elementary, 687 children ride buses to school. About how many children ride buses if the number is rounded to the nearest hundred?

SCHOOL BUS

600	680	690	700	NH
F	G	H	J	K

10 Dottie sewed buttons on a shirt. There were 5 buttons on each card. She had 3 cards. How many buttons did Dottie sew on the shirt?

18	15	8	2	NH
A	B	C	D	E

11 Suki bought a ball for $3.55. She paid $0.20 tax.

$3.55

How much did Suki spend altogether?

$3.75.

12 Hsu paid $3.29 for a box of paints.

Sarah

PAINTS

$3.29

3.29
1.00
79

She gave the clerk five $1.00 bills.

THE UNITED STATES OF AMERICA
ONE DOLLAR

If there was no tax, how much change should Hsu receive?

Sarah

$2.81	$2.71	$1.81	$1.71	NH
F	G	H	J	K

13 Mr. Jones had to drive 380 miles to visit his brother. He had driven 189 miles by lunch. How many more miles does Mr. Jones have to drive?

- Ⓐ 211
- Ⓑ 201
- Ⓒ 191
- Ⓓ 91
- Ⓔ NH

380
-189
191

14 Phoebe had saved $8.50. She earned $3.50 feeding a neighbor's cat. How much money does Phoebe have in all?

$12.50	$12.00	$11.50	$11.00	NH
F	G	H	J	K

STOP

Test 2: Math Problem Solving

Sample A

Which number belongs in the box to make the number sentence correct?

$$\boxed{\square \times 1 = 24}$$

- (A) 2
- (B) 4
- (C) 23
- (D) 24

For questions 1-44, darken the circle for the correct answer, or write in the answer.

1 Harvey has 1,354 baseball cards in his collection. What is the value of the 3 in 1,354?

- (A) three thousand
- (B) three hundred
- (C) thirty
- (D) three

2 The students in Mr. Lee's class are reading books. The table shows the fraction of the book each student has read.

Name	Amount Read
Amy	$\frac{1}{5}$
Jay	$\frac{1}{4}$
Meiko	$\frac{1}{8}$
Ross	$\frac{1}{3}$

Which student read the most?

- (F) Amy
- (G) Jay
- (H) Meiko
- (J) Ross

3 Which is another way to write 300 + 50 + 2?

- (A) 352
- (B) 3,052
- (C) 30,502
- (D) 300,502

4 Which number sentence is in the same fact family as

$$\boxed{11 - 4 = 7}\ ?$$

- (F) 11 + 4 = 15
- (G) 7 + 4 = 11
- (H) 7 - 4 = 3
- (J) 7 × 4 = 28

5 Which is another name for eight thousand four hundred ninety-two?

- (A) 8,492
- (B) 80,492
- (C) 84,920
- (D) 840,092

6 Andy has an odd number of coins in his coin collection. Which is Andy's coin collection?

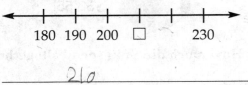

- (F)
- (G)
- (H)
- (J)

7 Which number belongs in the box on the number line?

180 190 200 □   230

210

8 Which muffin pan is $\frac{1}{2}$ empty?

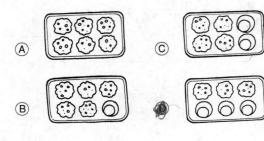

- (A)
- (B)
- (C)
- (D)

▶ GO ON

9 Which number belongs in the box to make the number sentence correct?

$$6 \times \square = 7 \times 6$$

Ⓕ 42

Ⓗ 7

Ⓖ 13

Ⓙ 4

10 What fraction of the shape is shaded?

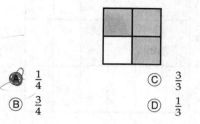

Ⓐ $\frac{1}{4}$

Ⓒ $\frac{3}{3}$

Ⓑ $\frac{3}{4}$

Ⓓ $\frac{1}{3}$

11 The table shows the number of lunches sold in the cafeteria in one week.

Day	Lunches
Monday	298
Tuesday	329
Wednesday	285
Thursday	351
Friday	246

On which day were the most lunches sold?

Ⓕ Monday

Ⓗ Wednesday

Ⓖ Tuesday

Ⓙ Thursday

12 The pet store sells 4 fish for $1. What is the missing number that completes the pattern in the chart?

Fish to Buy	
Number of Dollars	Number of Fish
$ 2	8
$ 3	12
$ 4	?
$ 5	20

Ⓐ 16

Ⓒ 13

Ⓑ 14

Ⓓ 4

13 The chart below shows how much 4 bags of cookies weigh.

Cookie	Weight
Chocolate chip	2.2 lbs.
Fruit bars	1.7 lbs.
Ginger snaps	2.5 lbs.
Oatmeal	1.9 lbs.

Which cookie bag weighs the least?

Ⓕ Chocolate chip

Ⓗ Ginger snaps

Ⓖ Fruit bars

Ⓙ Oatmeal

14 Which of these shows the missing piece in the figure?

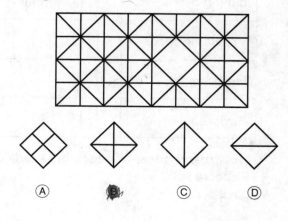

Ⓐ   Ⓑ   Ⓒ   Ⓓ

GO ON

15 The table shows rainfall amounts in 4 cities in Texas.

City	Rain Per Year
Austin	30 inches
Dallas	35 inches
Fort Worth	35 inches
Houston	42 inches

Which two cities together receive a total of 72 inches of rain a year?

Ⓕ Austin and Dallas

Ⓖ Dallas and Houston

Ⓗ Fort Worth and Dallas

Ⓙ Austin and Houston

16 What is the missing number that completes the pattern in the boxes?

19	15	11	7	

Ⓐ 8

Ⓑ 6

Ⓒ 4

Ⓓ 3

17 The tally chart keeps track of the boxes of seeds Rebecca sells.

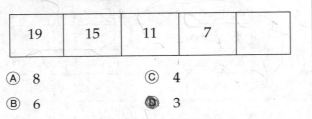

Kinds of Seeds	Boxes Sold
Flower Seeds	卌 卌
Vegetable Seeds	卌 |||
Herb Seeds	卌	
Birdseed	||||

How many boxes of vegetable seeds did Rebecca sell?

Ⓕ 2

Ⓖ 4

Ⓗ 6

Ⓙ 8

The graph below shows the shoes students are wearing in Mrs. Fryman's class. Study the graph and answer questions 18 through 20.

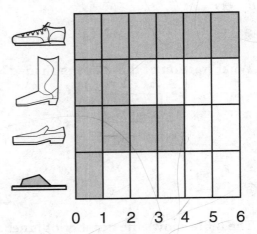

0 1 2 3 4 5 6

18 How many students are wearing sandals and boots?

Ⓐ 1

Ⓑ 2

Ⓒ 3

Ⓓ 6

19 Which category shows the shoes that 4 students are wearing?

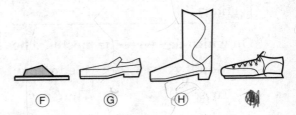

Ⓕ   Ⓖ   Ⓗ   Ⓙ

20 How many more students are wearing shoes than boots?

_____ 8

_____

_____

GO ON

21 What shape does the ball have?

Ⓐ pyramid

Ⓑ cone

Ⓒ sphere

Ⓓ cube

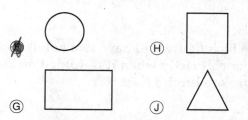

22 What is the location of the 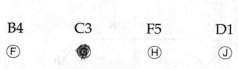 ?

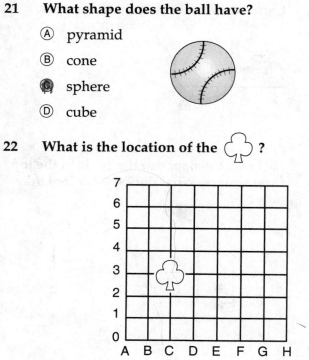

B4   C3   F5   D1

Ⓕ   Ⓖ   Ⓗ   Ⓙ

23 Look at the numbered shapes. Which two figures are exactly the same in size and shape?

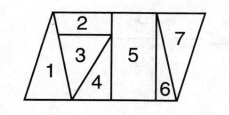

Ⓐ 1 and 4

Ⓑ 2 and 5

Ⓒ 1 and 7

Ⓓ 4 and 6

24 These shapes were picked out of a box.

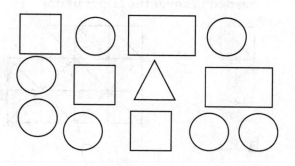

If one more shape is picked from the box, which shape will it most likely be?

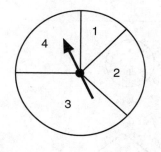

Ⓕ   Ⓗ

Ⓖ   Ⓙ

25 Terry is playing a game with the spinner. Which number will the next spin most likely show?

_____

_____

_____

_____

_____

26 How many of the smaller figures are needed to cover the larger figure?

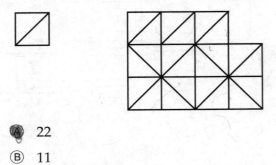

Ⓐ 22

Ⓑ 11

Ⓒ 10

Ⓓ 7

27 Which figure will have two halves that match exactly when it is folded on the broken line?

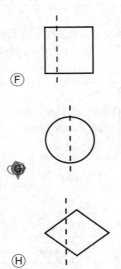

Ⓕ

Ⓖ

Ⓗ

Ⓙ

28 Carlos drew a car on a sheet of paper.

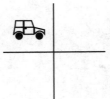

He turns the paper so the car is in the top, right square. What does the car look like now?

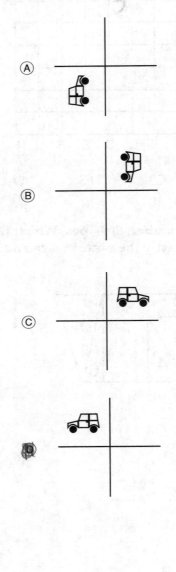

Ⓐ

Ⓑ

Ⓒ

Ⓓ

▶GO ON

29 Charles found some change in his gym bag. What is the value of the money shown?

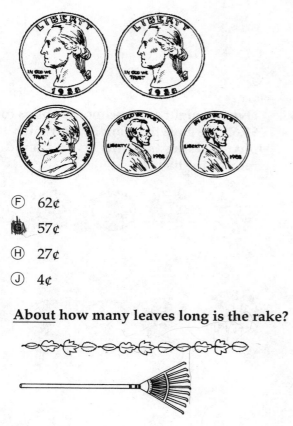

- Ⓕ 62¢
- Ⓖ 57¢
- Ⓗ 27¢
- Ⓙ 4¢

30 <u>About</u> how many leaves long is the rake?

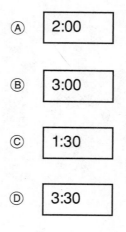

- Ⓐ 12
- Ⓑ 10
- Ⓒ 9
- Ⓓ 8

31 Which unit of measurement is best to use to describe the height of a tree?

- Ⓕ inches
- Ⓖ feet
- Ⓗ pounds
- Ⓙ miles

32 The table below shows the number of sports cards Artie has in his collection.

Sports Card Collection

Sport	Number of Cards
Football	16
Basketball	13
Baseball	29
Soccer	18
Hockey	9

Which two categories added together equal the number of baseball cards?

_____

_____

_____

_____

33 The time is now 9:30. What time will it be four and one-half hours from now?

- Ⓐ 2:00
- Ⓑ 3:00
- Ⓒ 1:30
- Ⓓ 3:30

⯈ **GO ON** ⯈

75

34 How many small squares in all are needed to fill the large square shown below?

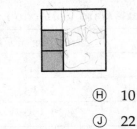

(F) 7   (H) 10

(G) 9   (J) 22

35 The forest animals come to drink the water in a pond. Which animal lives the shortest distance from the pond?

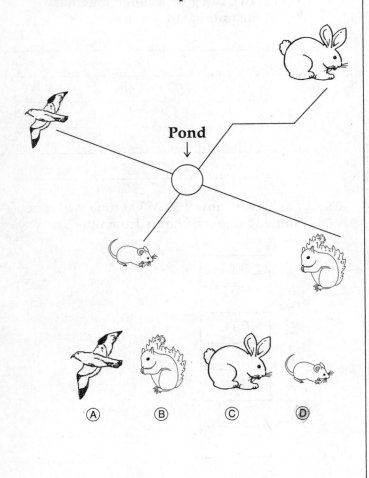

Pond

(A)   (B)   (C)   (D)

36 Barbara and Ronnie are raking leaves. What is the temperature like outside?

(F) 21°

(G) 32°

(H) 55°

(J) 98°

37 Dylan bought some school supplies for $1.67. He gave the clerk $2.00. Which picture shows the coins Dylan should receive in change?

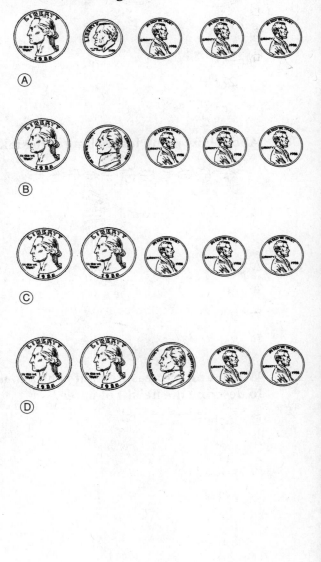

(A)

(B)

(C)

(D)

▶ GO ON

76

38 The table shows the number of animals entered in a farm show.

Animal	Number of Animals
Cow	29
Goats	22
Pigs	32
Sheep	19

<u>About</u> how many animals were entered altogether?

F 100

G 80

H 70

J 40

39 Jared wants to buy a book for $3 and a football for $10. How much money does he need?

A $1

B $5

C $10

D $20

40 What number is in the square, is outside the circle, and is an even number?

F 2

G 6

H 9

J 10

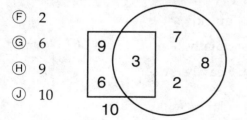

41 Yoshi put 2 stamps on each letter she was going to mail. What do you need to know to find out how many stamps Yoshi used?

A how many letters she was going to mail

B how long the envelopes were

C how many stamps she bought

D how much the stamps cost

42 Alice has 5 more tickets than Claire. Claire has 3 fewer tickets than Melba. Melba has 7 tickets. How many tickets does Alice have?

F 15

G 9

H 6

J 1

43 What temperature is shown on the thermometer?

A 52°

B 54°

C 58°

D 60°

44 Mark has 4 vases. He put 7 flowers in each vase. Write a number sentence that shows how to find the total number of flowers Mark used.

_____

_____

_____

_____

_____

Listening for Word Meanings

Directions: Darken the circle for the word or words that best answer the question you hear.

> **TRY THIS**
>
> Listen for key words in each sentence. Then listen carefully as each answer choice is read aloud. Decide which answer choice matches the key words and makes the most sense in the sentence.

Sample A

- Ⓐ forget about it
- Ⓑ guess about it
- Ⓒ ignore it
- Ⓓ think about it

> **THINK IT THROUGH**
>
> The correct answer is <u>D</u>, <u>think about it</u>. The key words in the sentence are <u>I'd like my parents to consider</u>. Other words that mean almost the same as consider are <u>think about it</u>.

1
- Ⓐ goes down
- Ⓑ drifts
- Ⓒ expands
- Ⓓ spreads out

2
- Ⓕ tasty
- Ⓖ healthy
- Ⓗ filling
- Ⓙ sickening

3
- Ⓐ worried
- Ⓑ calm
- Ⓒ thrilled
- Ⓓ forgetful

4
- Ⓕ very little
- Ⓖ extreme
- Ⓗ moderate
- Ⓙ limited

5
- Ⓐ small
- Ⓑ quick
- Ⓒ neat
- Ⓓ tired

6
- Ⓕ slowly
- Ⓖ quickly
- Ⓗ quietly
- Ⓙ heavily

7
- Ⓐ glance
- Ⓑ stare
- Ⓒ gaze
- Ⓓ observe

8
- Ⓕ fee
- Ⓖ allowance
- Ⓗ discount
- Ⓙ loan

Directions: Listen carefully to the story as it is read aloud. Darken the circle for the word or words that best answer the question.

| TRY THIS | Form a picture of the story in your mind. Listen carefully for details given in the story. |

Sample A

Ⓐ blow up balloons

Ⓑ fly a kite

Ⓒ blow whistles

Ⓓ run a race

THINK IT THROUGH

The correct answer is <u>B</u>, <u>fly a kite</u>. The story tells you that Josh bought a kite to fly with his big brother. He bought some balloons and whistles for his birthday party. The story does not mention running a race.

 STOP

1
Ⓐ mosquito
Ⓑ spider
Ⓒ butterfly
Ⓓ lady bug

2
Ⓕ leaves
Ⓖ silky thread
Ⓗ cotton
Ⓙ twigs

3
Ⓐ fried eggs and biscuits
Ⓑ cheese sandwiches
Ⓒ pancakes
Ⓓ scrambled eggs and toast

4
Ⓕ milk
Ⓖ butter
Ⓗ water
Ⓙ bread

5
Ⓐ today
Ⓑ seven days ago
Ⓒ last month
Ⓓ two weeks ago

6
Ⓕ smile
Ⓖ talk
Ⓗ eat
Ⓙ sleep

7
Ⓐ carrots
Ⓑ lettuce
Ⓒ grass
Ⓓ cabbage

8
Ⓕ frog
Ⓖ rabbit
Ⓗ little boy
Ⓙ farmer

STOP

Test

Sample A

 Ⓐ put in

 Ⓑ tear out

 Ⓒ plan

 Ⓓ order

STOP

1 Ⓐ solve

 Ⓑ tie again

 Ⓒ create

 Ⓓ convince

2 Ⓕ friendly

 Ⓖ interesting

 Ⓗ dull

 Ⓙ talkative

3 Ⓐ tune

 Ⓑ orchestra

 Ⓒ noise

 Ⓓ singer

4 Ⓕ careful

 Ⓖ hurried

 Ⓗ foolish

 Ⓙ important

5 Ⓐ talk about her

 Ⓑ admire her

 Ⓒ look like her

 Ⓓ try to act like her

6 Ⓕ common

 Ⓖ beautiful

 Ⓗ expensive

 Ⓙ unusual

7 Ⓐ mumble

 Ⓑ laugh

 Ⓒ shout

 Ⓓ whisper

8 Ⓕ skillful

 Ⓖ smooth

 Ⓗ awkward

 Ⓙ dangerous

9 Ⓐ make something new

 Ⓑ find something new

 Ⓒ notice something new

 Ⓓ misplace something new

10 Ⓕ take care of

 Ⓖ become tired of

 Ⓗ make fun of

 Ⓙ cherish

11 Ⓐ banker

 Ⓑ teacher

 Ⓒ doctor

 Ⓓ lawyer

12 Ⓕ careful

 Ⓖ unconcerned

 Ⓗ afraid

 Ⓙ worried

►GO ON►

Sample B

- Ⓐ park
- Ⓑ museum
- Ⓒ store
- Ⓓ library

STOP

13
- Ⓐ play
- Ⓑ costume
- Ⓒ mask
- Ⓓ race

14
- Ⓕ dragon
- Ⓖ evil queen
- Ⓗ prince
- Ⓙ princess

15
- Ⓐ raincoat
- Ⓑ winter coat
- Ⓒ sweater
- Ⓓ dress

16
- Ⓕ "A Rainy Day"
- Ⓖ "Fun at Summer Camp"
- Ⓗ "The Best Breakfast"
- Ⓙ "Carmela's Problem"

17
- Ⓐ loving
- Ⓑ foolish
- Ⓒ sad
- Ⓓ afraid

18
- Ⓕ washes the dishes
- Ⓖ makes her bed
- Ⓗ walks the dog
- Ⓙ does her homework

19
- Ⓐ Gloria washes the dishes.
- Ⓑ Gloria takes out the trash.
- Ⓒ Gloria makes her bed.
- Ⓓ Gloria helps her mother cook.

20
- Ⓕ the kite can fly
- Ⓖ the kite won't blow away
- Ⓗ you can decorate the kite
- Ⓙ you can catch the kite

21
- Ⓐ tin
- Ⓑ cloth
- Ⓒ paper
- Ⓓ wood

22
- Ⓕ throw away more trash
- Ⓖ learn how to pollute
- Ⓗ pick up trash
- Ⓙ do not be concerned about it

23
- Ⓐ bottles
- Ⓑ pollution
- Ⓒ newspapers
- Ⓓ cans

STOP

Prewriting, Composing, and Editing

Directions: Darken the circle for the correct answer to each question, or write in the answer.

TRY THIS | Pretend that you are writing each sentence. Use the rules you have learned for capitalization, punctuation, and writing clear, correct sentences.

Rosalina's Trip

Rosalina and her family went to Canada on vacation. They went to many places and had a great time. Rosalina wanted to tell her friend about her trip. So she wrote her a letter.

Sample A

Dear Debbie,
    I want to tell you about the great time I had
(1)
in Canada. We visited many places. I liked
         (2)   **(3)**
visiting Niagara Falls the best. My friend had
           (4)
a great time in Hawaii.

Which sentence does <u>not</u> belong in Rosalina's letter?

Ⓐ 1
Ⓑ 2
Ⓒ 3
Ⓓ 4

THINK IT THROUGH | The correct answer is <u>D</u>, <u>4</u>. This sentence does not tell about the topic of the paragraph, which is a vacation in Canada.

STOP

Here is the next part of Rosalina's letter.
    In <u>Ontario, canada,</u> we visited the
(5)
Welland Ship Canal. We watched a
              (6)
huge ship travel through the canal.

1   Write <u>Ontario, canada</u> correctly.

_____

_____

_____

_____

►GO ON

The Whale

Alfred's teacher wanted the students in the class to write a report about their favorite animal. Alfred's favorite animal is the whale. So Alfred decided to write his paper about the whale.

Alfred found the book *The Whale* in the library. Use the Table of Contents from this book to answer questions 5–7.

Table of Contents

2 Alfred put these words in alphabetical *(ABC)* order so he could find them more quickly in the dictionary. Which list is correct?

Ⓐ flippers–flukes–fins–fat

Ⓑ fat–flukes–fins–flippers

Ⓒ fat–fins–flippers–flukes

Ⓓ fins–fat–flippers–flukes

3 If Alfred wanted to find the meaning of the word *fluke*, where should he look first?

Ⓕ a dictionary

Ⓖ an encyclopedia

Ⓗ an atlas

Ⓙ a language arts book

4 Where could Alfred probably find the most information about whales?

Ⓐ a newspaper

Ⓑ an encyclopedia

Ⓒ a dictionary

Ⓓ a language arts book

5 Information about what whales eat begins on page

_____

_____

_____

6 In which chapter can Alfred find information about the way whales speak to one another?

3	4	5	6
Ⓕ	Ⓖ	Ⓗ	Ⓙ

7 Alfred can find information about the food that whales eat in Chapter—

2	3	4	6
Ⓐ	Ⓑ	Ⓒ	Ⓓ

Here is the first part of Alfred's report. Read it carefully. Then answer questions 8–11.

The Whale

It was easy to choose my favorite animal. It is the whale.
(1)   **(2)**

Jerry's favorite animal is the tiger. Did you know that whales did
(3)   **(4)**

not always live in the ocean? Millions of years ago, whales were
(5)

land animals. Walked around on four legs. They lived near the
(6)   **(7)**

oceans. They hunted in the waters near the shore. In time, the
(8)   **(9)**

whales went deeper into the sea. They began to feel more at
(10)

home in the ocean than on land. They became whales as we
(11)

know them today.

---

8 **Which group of words is not a complete sentence? Write the number of the group of words.**

_____

_____

_____

_____

_____

9 **What is the best way to write sentence 5?**

Ⓕ The whales millions of years ago were land animals.

Ⓖ The whales were millions of years ago land animals.

Ⓗ Land animals were whales millions of years ago.

Ⓙ As it is written.

10 **Which sentence does not belong in Alfred's report?**

1	3	5	7
Ⓐ	Ⓑ	Ⓒ	Ⓓ

11 **What is the best way to combine sentences 7 and 8 without changing their meaning?**

Ⓕ Living near the ocean, they hunted in waters near the shore.

Ⓖ They lived near the oceans and hunted in the waters near the shore.

Ⓗ They hunted near the shore and lived near the ocean.

Ⓙ They lived and hunted near the waters by the oceans.

 GO ON

Here is the next part of Alfred's report. This part has groups of words underlined. Read this part carefully. Then answer questions 12–15.

Whales can be found in all the <u>oceans of the world!</u> Some
(12)   (13)
whales live in water so deep that they are almost never seen.

Other whales live close to shore, so they're seen often. <u>Most</u>
(14)   (15)
<u>whales travels</u> from place to place. <u>They moves during</u>
(16)
<u>different times</u> of the year. Whales feed in the cold waters
(17)
near the North and South Poles for part of the year. <u>Ther'es</u>
(18)
<u>much more food</u> for whales there than in warmer waters.

Whales travel to warmer waters to have their babies.
(19)

---

12   In sentence 12, <u>oceans of the world!</u> is best written—

Ⓐ oceans of the world?

Ⓑ oceans of the world.

Ⓒ oceans of the world,

Ⓓ As it is written.

13   In sentence 15, <u>Most whales travels</u> is best written—

Ⓕ Most whales travel

Ⓖ Most whales traveling

Ⓗ Most whales traveled

Ⓙ As it is written.

14   In sentence 16, <u>They moves during different times</u> is best written—

Ⓐ They moved during different times

Ⓑ They move'd during different times

Ⓒ They move during different times

Ⓓ As it is written.

15   In sentence 18, <u>Ther'es much more food</u> is best written—

Ⓕ Theres' much more food

Ⓖ There's much more food

Ⓗ The'res much more food

Ⓙ As it is written.

GO ON

Time to go Camping!

Millie and her family go camping every summer. This year they will go with Millie's cousin Tara and her family. Millie decides to write Tara a letter to help her get ready for camping.

16 If Millie wanted to learn more about how to write a letter, she should look in—

Ⓐ a language arts book.

Ⓑ a dictionary.

Ⓒ an atlas.

Ⓓ an encyclopedia.

Millie made a list of things that Tara should bring for camping. Use her list to answer question 17.

Supplies For Camping

1. a tent
2. a warm sleeping bag
3. a flashlight
4. food for three days
5. plates, cups, spoons, forks, and knives
6. some snacks
7.

17 Which of these is <u>not</u> something Millie should list as number 7?

Ⓕ marshmallows to roast

Ⓖ nice jewelry to wear

Ⓗ a bucket to put out a campfire

Ⓙ a cooler to keep food cold

While Millie was writing her letter, she needed to check some words in the dictionary.

18 What definition best fits the word <u>trail</u> as used in the sentence below? Write the definition.

We went for a walk on the <u>trail</u>.

_____

_____

_____

_____

▶ GO ON

Here is the first page of Millie's letter. Read the letter carefully. Then answer questions 19–21.

Dear Tara,

I'm so glad that you will be able to go camping with us. I
(1)   (2)
can't wait! I know that you have never gone camping. So I
         (3)   (4)
want to tell you about it. Going camping is so much fun. You'll
                  (5)   (6)
get to be outside for three whole days. You'll get to eat outside.
                                              (7)
We'll cook food on a stove. We'll cook over a fire. At night you
(8)   (9)   (10)
can see thousands of stars in the sky. Sleeping in a tent is also
                                       (11)
a lot of fun. All the cousins will be able to sleep in the same tent.
         (12)

19 **What is the best way to combine sentences 8 and 9 without changing their meaning?**

Ⓐ We'll cook food on a stove, we'll cook over a fire.

Ⓑ On a stove and over a fire we'll cook food.

Ⓒ On a stove we'll cook food and over a fire we'll cook food.

Ⓓ We'll cook food on a stove and over a fire.

20 **What is the topic sentence of this paragraph?**

_____

_____

_____

_____

_____

21 **What is the best way to write sentence 12?**

Ⓕ In the same tent all the cousins will get to sleep.

Ⓖ All the cousins in the same tent will get to sleep.

Ⓗ All the cousins. Will get to sleep in the same tent.

Ⓙ As it is written.

▶GO ON◀

Here is the next part of Millie's letter. This part has groups of words underlined. Read this part carefully. Then answer questions 22–25.

You need to get things ready for camping. Your parents will
(13)   (14)
bring the tent. You should <u>bring an warm sleeping bag</u>. You
(15)   (16)
should also bring a flashlight. It's so much fun to use flashlights
(17)
to walk around the camp at night. Make sure you <u>bring pots</u>
(18)
<u>pans, and dishes</u>. You'll need them to cook your food. Hot dogs
(19)   (20)
and hamburgers taste great when you're camping! Make sure
(21)
you <u>brought a lot of</u> marshmallows. We'll be roasting them over
(22)
the fire. I'm also going to bring some fruit and some granola bars.
(23)
You should bring some, too.
(24)

<u>sincerely yours,</u>
Millie

22 In sentence 15, <u>bring an warm sleeping bag</u> is best written—

Ⓐ brought an warm sleeping bag

Ⓑ bring a warm sleeping bag

Ⓒ brought a warm sleeping bag

Ⓓ As it is written.

23 In sentence 18, <u>bring pots pans, and dishes</u> is best written—

Ⓕ bring pots, pans, and dishes

Ⓖ bring pots pans and dishes

Ⓗ bring pots, pans and dishes

Ⓙ As it is written.

24 In sentence 21, <u>brought a lot of</u> is best written—

Ⓐ brings a lot of

Ⓑ bringing a lot of

Ⓒ bring a lot of

Ⓓ As it is written.

25 At the end of Millie's letter, <u>sincerely yours,</u> is best written—

Ⓕ Sincerely Yours,

Ⓖ Sincerely yours,

Ⓗ sincerely Yours,

Ⓙ As it is written.

STOP

Identifying Misspelled Words

Directions: Read each sentence carefully. If one of the words is misspelled, darken the circle for that word. If all the words are spelled correctly, then darken the circle for *No Mistake*.

TRY THIS	Read each sentence carefully. If you are not sure of an answer, first decide which answer choices are spelled correctly. Then see if you can recognize the misspelled word from your reading experience.

Sample A

May played a <u>livly</u> <u>tune</u> on her <u>piano</u>. <u>No mistake</u>
       Ⓐ Ⓑ   Ⓒ   Ⓓ

THINK IT THROUGH	The correct answer is <u>A</u>, for the first underlined word. All of the other words are spelled correctly. <u>Livly</u> should be spelled l-i-v-e-l-y. You should not drop the <u>e</u> when you add <u>-ly</u>.

---

1   In <u>sewing</u> <u>class</u> I am making an <u>aperun</u> for my mom. <u>No mistake</u>
       Ⓐ   Ⓑ   Ⓒ   Ⓓ

2   We saw some <u>unusual</u> <u>butterflies</u> in the <u>woods</u>. <u>No mistake</u>
          Ⓕ   Ⓖ   Ⓗ   Ⓙ

3   Don told the <u>scaryest</u> <u>ghost</u> story at <u>camp</u>. <u>No mistake</u>
          Ⓐ   Ⓑ   Ⓒ   Ⓓ

4   The car <u>startd</u> to <u>slide</u> on the icy <u>highway</u>. <u>No mistake</u>
         Ⓕ   Ⓖ   Ⓗ   Ⓙ

5   The <u>magical</u> king <u>granted</u> the shoemaker three <u>wishs</u>. <u>No mistake</u>
      Ⓐ   Ⓑ   Ⓒ   Ⓓ

Sample A

Go Fly a Kite

Leon's scout troop has entered a kite contest. Leon knows how to make and fly a kite. He wants to write a paper to help the other scouts get ready for the contest.

Leon wants to find out when the kite contest in his city will take place. He should look in—

Ⓐ an atlas.

Ⓑ an encyclopedia.

Ⓒ a dictionary.

Ⓓ a newspaper.

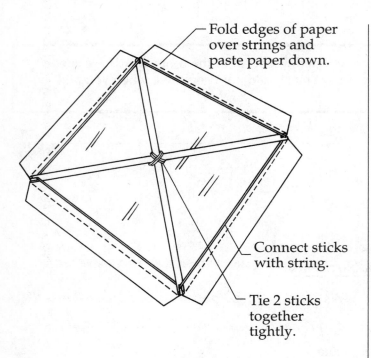

Fold edges of paper over strings and paste paper down.

Connect sticks with string.

Tie 2 sticks together tightly.

1 Here is a sketch Leon drew of a kite. How will it best help him to write his paper?

Ⓐ It will help him picture what kind of paper to use.

Ⓑ It will help him picture how to put the kite together.

Ⓒ It will help him remember a kite contest he once entered.

Ⓓ It will help him decide to enter the kite contest.

2 Leon found the book *How To Fly a Kite*. Where in the book should he look to find the author's name?

Ⓕ Chapter 1

Ⓖ the title page

Ⓗ the table of contents

Ⓙ the index

3 If Leon wanted to find out when kites were first made, where should he look?

Ⓐ a dictionary

Ⓑ an atlas

Ⓒ a language arts book

Ⓓ an encyclopedia

4 Where should Leon look to find the meaning of the word <u>fasten</u>?

_____

_____

_____

_____

_____

_____

_____

Here is the first part of Leon's paper. Read it carefully. Then answer questions 5–7.

How to Make a Kite

I'm going to tell you how to make a flat kite. Make sure that
(1)   **(2)**

you have two sticks, string, paper, and glue. Take the two sticks
                          (3)

and cross them into an *X*. Use the string to tie the sticks together.
                (4)

Tie them tightly where the two sticks cross. Then add glue to make
(5)   **(6)**

sure the two sticks stay together. Around the ends of the sticks tie
                    (7)

a string. This will be the outer edge of the kite. Then cut a large
         (8)   **(9)**

piece of paper. Fold the edges of the paper over the string all
       (10)

around the kite. Use paste to glue the paper around the string.
               (11)

My sister made a beautiful kite.
(12)

---

5   **What is the topic sentence of this paragraph?**

    1   2   3   4

    Ⓕ   Ⓖ   Ⓗ   Ⓙ

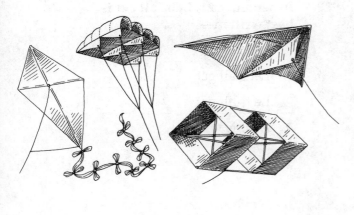

6   **What is the best way to write sentence 7?**

  Ⓐ   Around the ends of the sticks a string tie.

  Ⓑ   Tie a string around the ends of the sticks.

  Ⓒ   A string tie around the ends of the sticks.

  Ⓓ   As it is written.

7   **Which sentence does not belong in Leon's paper? Write the number.**

_____

_____

_____

_____

▶ **GO ON** ◀

Here is the next part of Leon's paper. This part has groups of words underlined. Read this part carefully. Then answer questions 8–11.

<u>The Kite Contest</u> will take place in April. The most important
(13)   **(14)**

thing to remember is that your kite has to fly. Then you can enter
                          (15)

your kite in three events. The first event will decide which kite is
                (16)

decorated the best. The judges will look at the colors and designs
                 (17)

you use. The second event will decide which kite can fly the
        (18)

highest. The judges will give you about ten minutes to get your
       (19)

kite <u>into the air!</u> The third event will decide how fast you can
            (20)

send out your kite to the end of the line <u>and reels it in again.</u>

<u>Lets' all get</u> busy and get our kites ready!
(21)

---

8   In sentence 13, <u>**The Kite Contest**</u> is best written—

     Ⓕ   The kite contest

     Ⓖ   The Kite contest

     Ⓗ   the kite Contest

     Ⓙ   As it is written.

9   In sentence 19, <u>into the air!</u> is best written—

     Ⓐ   into the air?

     Ⓑ   into the air,

     Ⓒ   into the air.

     Ⓓ   As it is written.

10   In sentence 20, <u>and reels it in again.</u> is best written—

     Ⓕ   and reel it in again.

     Ⓖ   and reeling it in again.

     Ⓗ   and reel's it in again.

     Ⓙ   As it is written.

11   In sentence 21, <u>Lets' all get</u> is best written—

     Ⓐ   Lets all get

     Ⓑ   Let's all get

     Ⓒ   Le'ts all get

     Ⓓ   As it is written.

▶ GO ON

Learning About the Moon

Mary and her class went on a field trip to a planetarium. Her teacher wanted each student to write a paper and tell about one thing they learned. Mary decided to write about the moon.

12 **Why is Mary writing the paper?**

Ⓕ to tell about the moon and planets

Ⓖ to ask her parents to go to the planetarium

Ⓗ to describe the moon

Ⓙ to tell what she learned at the planetarium

13 **Mary put these words in alphabetical (ABC) order so she could find them more quickly in the dictionary. Which list is correct?**

Ⓐ meteors – moonrise – motion – mountains

Ⓑ moonrise – mountains – meteors – motion

Ⓒ mountains – motion – moonrise – meteors

Ⓓ meteors – motion – moonrise – mountains

Mary found the book *The Moon* in the library. Use the Table of Contents and Index from the book to answer questions 14–16.

Table of Contents

Index

14 **In which chapter could Mary find information about the astronauts who walked on the moon?**

2　　　3　　　4　　　5
Ⓕ　　Ⓖ　　Ⓗ　　Ⓙ

15 **Mary can find information about moon craters on page—**

8　　　23　　　25　　　43
Ⓐ　　Ⓑ　　Ⓒ　　Ⓓ

16 **Information about how the moon came to be can be found in Chapter—**

_____

_____

_____

_____

GO ON

Here is the first part of Mary's report. Read it carefully. Then answer questions 17–20.

Learning About the Moon

I really enjoyed going to the planetarium. I learned a lot about
(1)   (2)
the moon. The moon is smaller than Earth. Jupiter is the largest
(3)   (4)
planet. The moon is about 238,000 miles away from Earth. That's
(5)   (6)
not very far when you're talking about outer space. You cannot
(7)
live on the moon. The moon has no water. It has no air. During
(8)   (9)   (10)
the day the moon is hot. Enough to fry an egg. At night, the
(11)   (12)
moon is colder than the North Pole. The moon is covered with
(13)
dust–covered flat land. It also has many different sizes of craters.
(14)

17 Which of these is <u>not</u> a complete sentence?

   5   7   9   11
   Ⓕ   Ⓖ   Ⓗ   Ⓙ

18 What is the best way to combine sentences 8 and 9 without changing their meaning?

  Ⓐ The moon, which has no air, has no water.

  Ⓑ The moon has no water and the moon has no air.

  Ⓒ The moon has no water and no air.

  Ⓓ The moon having no water has no air.

19 Which sentence does <u>not</u> belong in Mary's paper?

   2   4   6   8
   Ⓕ   Ⓖ   Ⓗ   Ⓙ

20 Which of these could be added after sentence 14?

  Ⓐ Some of the craters are old volcanoes.

  Ⓑ Some planets have more than one moon.

  Ⓒ Jamie liked visiting the planetarium, too.

  Ⓓ Earth is the third planet from the sun.

 GO ON

Here is the next part of Mary's report. This part has groups of words underlined. Read this part carefully. Then answer questions 21–24.

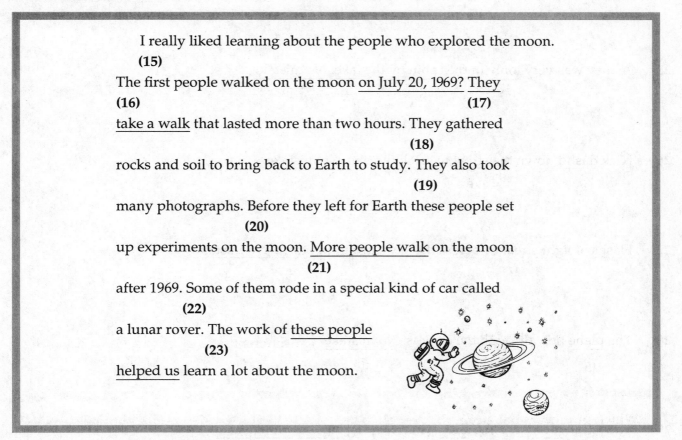

I really liked learning about the people who explored the moon.
(15)

The first people walked on the moon <u>on July 20, 1969? They</u>
(16)   (17)

<u>take a walk</u> that lasted more than two hours. They gathered
(18)

rocks and soil to bring back to Earth to study. They also took
(19)

many photographs. Before they left for Earth these people set
(20)

up experiments on the moon. <u>More people walk</u> on the moon
(21)

after 1969. Some of them rode in a special kind of car called
(22)

a lunar rover. The work of <u>these people</u>
(23)

<u>helped us</u> learn a lot about the moon.

---

21 In sentence 16, <u>on July 20, 1969?</u> is best written—

   Ⓕ on July 20, 1969,

   Ⓖ on July 20, 1969.

   Ⓗ On July 20, 1969?

   Ⓙ As it is written.

22 In sentence 17, <u>They take a walk</u> is best written—

   Ⓐ They taking a walk

   Ⓑ They takes a walk

   Ⓒ They took a walk

   Ⓓ As it is written.

23 In sentence 21, <u>More people walk</u> is best written—

   Ⓕ More people walked

   Ⓖ More people is walking

   Ⓗ More people walks

   Ⓙ As it is written.

24 In sentence 23, <u>these people helped us</u> is best written—

   Ⓐ these people helping us

   Ⓑ these people is helped us

   Ⓒ these people has helping us

   Ⓓ As it is written.

▶ GO ON ▶

For questions 25–32, read each sentence carefully. If one of the words is misspelled, darken the circle for that word. If all the words are spelled correctly, then darken the circle for *No mistake*.

25 Ashley was very lonly in the cabin by the lake. No mistake
               (F)   (G)   (H)   (J)

26 Nick dashd down the street to catch the bus. No mistake
     (A)   (B)   (C)   (D)

27 Flashs of light streaked across the sky during the storm. No mistake
   (F)   (G)   (H)   (J)

28 The plane flew through the clowds. No mistake
     (A)   (B)   (C)   (D)

29 The kitten raced into the alley when the dog barked. No mistake
       (F)   (G)   (H)   (J)

30 Bob walked to the store to buy vegetables. No mistake
      (A)   (B)   (C)   (D)

31 Phil enjoys reading advenchure stories. No mistake
        (F)   (G) (H)   (J)

32 This is the greasyest pan I've ever washed! No mistake
     (A) (B)   (C)   (D)

STOP

Reading Comprehension

Sample A

Cathy's Vacation Plans

Cathy is excited about going camping with her family this summer. They plan to go to the Grand Canyon where they will stay for two weeks.

How long will Cathy's family camp?

- Ⓐ two days
- Ⓑ two weeks
- Ⓒ two months
- Ⓓ the entire summer

For questions 1–32, read each story and the questions that follow. Then darken the circle for the correct answer to each question, or write in the answer.

How to Plant a Tree

Planting a tree is a good way to clean the air, provide a home for birds, and make the world more beautiful. You will need a tree, a shovel, and *mulch.*

First, choose a good spot for the tree. It should not be too close to a building or other trees or beneath telephone wires. Dig a two-feet-deep hole with sloping sides.

Second, remove or cut away the container that the tree is in. Pick up the tree by the root ball, not the trunk, and set it in the hole. Then fill the hole with dirt around the root ball. When the hole is a little more than half full, fill the hole with water and stir the mud with your shovel. This will settle the soil and remove air pockets. Then finish filling in the hole with dirt.

Last, place *mulch,* or leaves, straw, or bark, around the tree. Water the tree, and step back to admire your work!

1 Planting a tree will do all of the following except—

- Ⓐ make the world more beautiful.
- Ⓑ save water.
- Ⓒ clean the air.
- Ⓓ provide a home for birds.

2 What can be used to make mulch?

_____

_____

_____

_____

 You have 30 minutes to complete this test.

When Grandma Was a Young Girl

Grandma has told me many stories about what it was like growing up on the farm when she was a girl. Her family lived ten miles from any neighbors. They had little money to buy food in a store. They had to grow most of their food on the farm. They raised cows and chickens for meat. They grew and then canned fruits and vegetables to last the whole winter. Grandma's family stored some of the food in an underground cellar to keep it from spoiling. They also had an underground spring near the house. The water was very cold. They stored milk, butter, and eggs in the spring to keep them fresh.

Grandma and her family had to work very hard. I am glad that we have cars and can go to the grocery store to buy our food.

3 The writer thinks that Grandma's life on the farm was—

- Ⓕ difficult.
- Ⓖ easy.
- Ⓗ fun.
- Ⓙ boring.

4 How did the family keep milk and butter fresh?

- Ⓐ They canned it.
- Ⓑ They stored it in a spring.
- Ⓒ They used a refrigerator.
- Ⓓ They kept it in a cellar.

5 Why did Grandma's family have to grow most of their food?

They didn't have enough money

6 Which question does the first paragraph answer?

- Ⓕ How big was the farm?
- Ⓖ What was the grandmother's favorite thing to do?
- Ⓗ How did the family get food?
- Ⓙ Where did the grandmother go to school?

All About Bees

Bees are always busy. Worker bees fly from flower to flower, and then they fly back to the beehive. There the worker bees make honey. They help the queen bee by building nests. They also clean the nests and take care of baby bees. The queen bee lays all the eggs for the beehive. The work that bees do is useful to people. Bees help plants grow in gardens and on farms. The sweet honey that bees make is delicious to eat.

7 Worker bees do all of the following except—

Ⓐ make honey.

Ⓑ lay eggs.

Ⓒ clean the nest.

Ⓓ take care of baby bees.

8 What job does the queen bee have?

lags all the eggs
g for their beehive

9 What is another good title for this story?

Ⓕ "Busy, Busy Bees"

Ⓖ "How Honey is Made"

Ⓗ "A Day in the Life of a Queen Bee"

Ⓙ "Why Bees Like Flowers"

10 How is the work that bees do useful to people?

Ⓐ Bees clean their own nests.

Ⓑ Bees help plants grow in gardens and on farms.

Ⓒ Bees are fun to watch.

Ⓓ Bees are always busy.

An Important Food

When you think of bread, what comes to mind? Do you think of a fresh loaf of white bread? Perhaps you picture a nice loaf of wheat bread. If you lived in another country, you might have a very different idea of bread. A boy or girl in Mexico would think of *tortillas*. These are flat, round breads made from corn. People in India would think of *chappatis*. These are heavy pieces of round bread that are fried.

Bread is one of the most important foods. It is eaten more than any other food. It is also eaten in more places than any other food.

Bread has been an important food for a very long time. The first bread was made about 12,000 years ago. People in the Middle East gathered the seeds of wild plants. They used the seeds to make flour. They mixed the flour with water. Then they baked it on hot rocks.

Later people learned how to plant seeds so they could grow their own wheat. People in Egypt learned that if they added yeast to the flour and water, it would make the bread rise. The Egyptians also learned to build ovens in which to bake the bread.

For hundreds of years, bread was made in the same way. But in time, people wanted a light bread. They learned that if flour was sifted through cloth, the rough pieces could be taken out. Then they would have white flour. From white flour, soft white bread could be made. For many years only rich people could buy white bread. Today many people like whole-wheat bread better than white bread. We know that the rough pieces of flour are good for us.

GO ON

11 You would probably find this story in a book called—

F   *Important Foods around the World.*

G   *Holidays in Many Places.*

H   *Foods from Mexico.*

J   *How to Grow Wheat.*

12 Who first added yeast to bread?

A   Egyptians

B   people in the Middle East

C   Germans

D   Mexicans

13 What are *chappatis*?

F   flat, round breads made of corn

G   sweet biscuits

H   heavy pieces of fried bread

J   soft, rye breads

14 To answer question 13, the reader should—

A   reread the first line of each paragraph.

B   reread the last paragraph of the story.

C   look for the word *chappatis* in the story.

D   reread the title of the story.

15 What is this story mainly about?

F   how to make bread

G   how to eat bread

H   types of flat bread

J   the history of bread

16 If the story continued, it would probably tell about—

A   ways bread is made today.

B   how to eat a healthful diet.

C   medicines made from plants.

D   favorite foods of children.

17 What question does the second paragraph answer?

F   How is bread made?

G   What food is eaten more than any other?

H   Who made the first bread?

J   What kind of bread do people like best?

18 What was bread first made from?

The flour was mixed with water they baked it in the rocks

Visiting Grandmother

Tino loves to visit his grandmother. He doesn't get to visit her very often because his family lives in a city that is six hours away. His grandmother lives in a big wooden house on a farm. It is old and looks like it has secret hiding places.

On the second Sunday of July, Tino's parents took him to his grandmother's. Since it was summer vacation, he was going to stay at Grandmother's for a whole month! His cousins Doug and Barbara would soon be arriving. They would also be staying at their grandmother's this summer.

A big porch wraps around two sides of the house. Tino sat in the porch swing. He could see the trees that circle the house. They had been planted as a *windbreak*. They protect the house from the wind and blowing dirt. The house is in the middle of a large, flat field.

Tino watched the dirt road that leads to the house. He couldn't wait for his cousins to get there! Doug was his age, and Barbara was a year younger. They always had fun together. Last summer they had spent one whole morning making a fort out of sacks of seed that they found in the barn. Then Uncle John had taken them on a tractor ride.

Tino remembered another time with his cousins. They had gone out to explore the fields. Tino touched an electric fence and got a shock. Then they found an old snakeskin. Nothing like that ever happened at home! Tino took the snakeskin to school and showed it to everyone.

Tino could smell the dinner that his mother and grandmother were cooking. He smelled ham, hot rolls, and pumpkin pie. It made him hungry.

Finally he saw a cloud of dust coming up the road. "They're here! They're here!" he shouted.

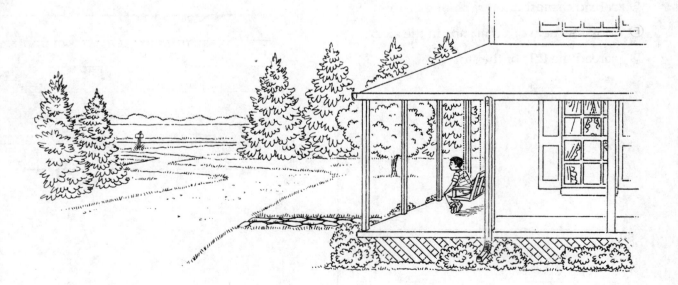

GO ON

19 After Tino's cousins arrive, what will probably happen next?

Ⓐ They will build a fort on the hill.

Ⓑ They will look for snakeskins.

Ⓒ They will climb the trees in their grandmother's yard.

Ⓓ They will eat dinner at their grandmother's house.

20 The story tells about Tino and his cousins doing all of the following <u>except</u>—

Ⓕ watching old movies.

Ⓖ taking a tractor ride.

Ⓗ finding a snakeskin.

Ⓙ making a fort from seed sacks.

21 How do you think Tino felt when he saw his cousins arriving?

Ⓐ He was worried.

Ⓑ He was excited.

Ⓒ He was angry.

Ⓓ He was sad.

22 Tino's grandmother lives in a—

Ⓕ brick house.

Ⓖ stone house.

Ⓗ wooden house.

Ⓙ new house.

23 What is meant by a *windbreak*?

A kind of a chair that swings

24 In order to answer question 23, the reader should—

Ⓐ read the title of the story again.

Ⓑ read the first paragraph again.

Ⓒ look in the story for the word *windbreak*.

Ⓓ read the last line of each paragraph again.

25 Tino's grandmother's house was—

Ⓕ on a hill.

Ⓖ in a valley.

Ⓗ in a field.

Ⓙ in a city.

26 These boxes show events that happened in the story.

Tino went to Grandmother's house.		Tino thought about another visit to Grandmother's.
1	**2**	**3**

What belongs in box 2?

Ⓐ Tino's cousins arrived at Grandmother's house.

Ⓑ Tino could smell dinner cooking.

Ⓒ Tino sat in the porch swing.

Ⓓ Tino saw a cloud of dust coming up the road.

▷GO ON▷

This poster was placed in the cafeteria at Taft Elementary School.

Help Our Environment!

April is "Help Our Environment!" month at Taft Elementary School. Students can help clean up our planet by collecting used cans, bottles, and newspapers. These things should be put in the recycling bins that have been placed in each classroom. Each class that fills its bin will get a "Clean Class" award. On Earth Day each student in these classes will get to plant a tree in the schoolyard. Let's all help make our school and our world a cleaner place!

27 According to the poster, all of the following activities will happen in April except—

Ⓕ collecting cans, bottles, and newspapers.

Ⓖ filling recycling bins.

Ⓗ planting trees.

Ⓙ taking a trip to the recycling center.

28 What will probably happen after the recycling bins are filled?

Ⓐ The materials will be taken to a recycling center.

Ⓑ The materials will be sent home with students.

Ⓒ The materials will be stored at the school.

Ⓓ The materials will be buried in the schoolyard.

29 Where was this sign posted?

Ⓕ at the neighborhood gym

Ⓖ at Taft Elementary School

Ⓗ at the supermarket

Ⓙ at East High School

30 The recycling bins are for—

Ⓐ bottles and cans.

Ⓑ bottles, plastic, and newspapers.

Ⓒ cans, plastic, and cardboard.

Ⓓ cans, bottles, and newspapers.

31 Who will get to plant trees?

Ⓕ classes who get a "Clean Class" award

Ⓖ students who buy a tree

Ⓗ students who read the most books

Ⓙ classes who make the best grades

32 When will the "Help Our Environment" program be held?

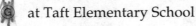 In April

STOP

Reading Vocabulary

Sample A

A parka is a kind of—

(A) warm jacket with a hood

(B) European folk dance

(C) dried meat

(D) sled

STOP

For questions 1-9, darken the circle for the word or words that have the <u>same</u> or <u>almost the same</u> meaning as the underlined word.

1   <u>Familiar</u> means—

(A) old

(B) beautiful

(C) known

(D) strange

2   A <u>lane</u> is most like a—

(F) ladder

(G) road

(H) shack

(J) race

3   To <u>cure</u> means to—

(A) heal

(B) clean

(C) study

(D) correct

4   A <u>tourist</u> is a kind of—

(F) judge   (H) teacher

(G) chair   (J) visitor

5   To <u>recall</u> something is to—

(A) prepare it

(B) clean it

(C) remember it

(D) include it

6   Something that is <u>precise</u> is—

(F) expensive

(G) exact

(H) rare

(J) safe

7   Something that is <u>soaked</u> is—

(A) wet

(B) dirty

(C) soiled

(D) wrinkled

8   A <u>jacket</u> is most like a—

(F) hat

(G) dress

(H) coat

(J) jar

9   A <u>kennel</u> is a place for—

(A) dogs

(B) airplanes

(C) plants

(D) cars

STOP

You have 15 minutes to complete this test.

105

Sample B

> Turn the key to make the car <u>run</u>.

In which sentence does <u>run</u> have the same meaning as it does in the sentence above?

(A) Water will always <u>run</u> downhill.

(B) This fan won't <u>run</u> any more.

(C) Li will <u>run</u> in the race today.

(D) I hit a <u>run</u> at our baseball game.

STOP

For questions 10–14, darken the circle for the sentence in which the underlined word means the same as it does in the sentence in the box.

10

> <u>Draw</u> a card and put it on the table.

In which sentence does <u>draw</u> have the same meaning as it does in the sentence above?

(F) We used horses to <u>draw</u> the wagon.

(G) Please <u>draw</u> a picture of a whale for me.

(H) The circus will <u>draw</u> a big crowd.

(J) Each of us will <u>draw</u> a number from the hat.

11

> We saw a boat sail on the <u>bay</u>.

In which sentence does <u>bay</u> have the same meaning as it does in the sentence above?

(A) The wolf began to <u>bay</u> at the moon.

(B) The winner was the <u>bay</u> horse.

(C) The water in that <u>bay</u> is icy.

(D) Put a <u>bay</u> leaf in the soup.

12

> I ate <u>part</u> of the pie.

In which sentence does <u>part</u> have the same meaning as it does in the sentence above?

(F) I won't <u>part</u> with my favorite jacket.

(G) Joe did <u>part</u> of the work.

(H) Trevor played the <u>part</u> of Peter Pan.

(J) The <u>part</u> in your hair is crooked.

13

> Always <u>check</u> your answers.

In which sentence does <u>check</u> have the same meaning as it does in the sentence above?

(A) Dad wrote a <u>check</u> for the clothes.

(B) I put a <u>check</u> beside my name.

(C) My marker is on the red <u>check</u>.

(D) <u>Check</u> to see if you have your ticket.

14

> We took a lunch <u>break</u> at noon.

In which sentence does <u>break</u> have the same meaning as it does in the sentence above?

(F) That old chain may <u>break</u>.

(G) At this ranch they <u>break</u> horses.

(H) If you are tired, take a <u>break</u>.

(J) The sun shone through a <u>break</u> in the clouds.

STOP

Sample C

That delicate fruit will bruise easily if it is bumped. Bruise means—

(A) mark

(B) hurt

(C) blossom

(D) taste

STOP

For questions 15–21, darken the circle for the word or words that give the meaning of the underlined word, or write in the answer.

15 He tried to navigate the space shuttle safely through the asteroid field. Navigate means—

(A) dock

(B) chase

(C) land

(D) steer

16 We were astounded by the magician's amazing tricks. Astounded means—

tricked

17 That organization works to preserve and protect the environment. Preserve means—

(F) clean up

(G) plant flowers

(H) hunt animals

(J) keep from being lost

18 He was in a hurry and had time for only a brief visit. Brief means—

(A) afternoon

(B) short

(C) casual

(D) lunch

19 He didn't want to lie so he gave him an honest answer. Honest means—

(F) truthful

(G) false

(H) strange

(J) long

20 She inscribed his name on the clay vase with a sharp pen. Inscribed means—

(A) wrote

(B) burned

(C) read

(D) underlined

21 If you plan to attend the party, please send a reply. Reply means—

(F) answer

(G) car

(H) invitation

(J) cake

Part 1: Math Problem Solving

Sample A

Which is another way to write 700 + 10 + 5?

Ⓐ 700,105   Ⓒ 7,150

Ⓑ 7,001   Ⓓ 715

For questions 1–43, darken the circle for the correct answer, or write in the answer.

1 Which number belongs on the number line at point C?

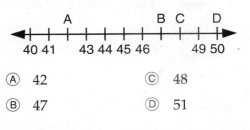

Ⓐ 42   Ⓒ 48

Ⓑ 47   Ⓓ 51

2 Jean has an even number of stamps in her stamp collection. Which is Jean's stamp collection?

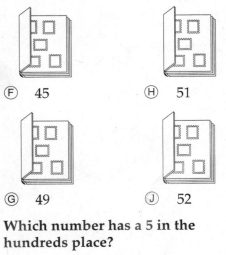

Ⓕ 45   Ⓗ 51

Ⓖ 49   Ⓙ 52

3 Which number has a 5 in the hundreds place?

Ⓐ 5,640   Ⓒ 56

Ⓑ 564   Ⓓ 5

4 The table shows the number of people who go to the movies during the week.

Day	Number of People
Monday	243
Tuesday	146
Wednesday	297
Thursday	185
Friday	324

On which day did the fewest number of people go to the movies?

Ⓕ Monday   Ⓗ Thursday

Ⓖ Tuesday   Ⓙ Friday

5 Which is another name for two thousand one hundred sixty?

Ⓐ 216   Ⓒ 2,160

Ⓑ 2,106   Ⓓ 21,600

6 The chart shows the number of students in grades one through four.

One	Two	Three	Four
290	163	249	312

Which of the following shows the grades listed in order from the fewest number of students to the most students?

Ⓕ Two, three, one, four

Ⓖ Three, two, one, four

Ⓗ Four, two, one, three

Ⓙ One, two, three, four

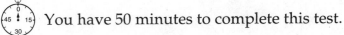

 You have 50 minutes to complete this test.

7 Which number sentence is in the same fact family as

$$9 - 6 = 3 \quad ?$$

Ⓐ $6 + 3 = 9$

Ⓑ $9 + 6 = 15$

Ⓒ $6 - 3 = 3$

Ⓓ $6 \geq 3 = 18$

8 Which number belongs in the box to make the number sentence correct?

$$2 \times \square = 9 \times 2$$

Ⓕ 2 Ⓗ 11

Ⓖ 9 Ⓙ 18

9 Which is another way to write 4 × 2?

Ⓐ $2 \times 2 \times 2 \times 2$

Ⓑ $8 + 2$

Ⓒ $4 + 2$

Ⓓ $2 + 2 + 2 + 2$

10 Which number belongs in the box to make the number sentence correct?

$$5 \times \square = 5$$

Ⓕ 10 Ⓗ 1

Ⓖ 5 Ⓙ 0

11 What fraction of the shape is not shaded?

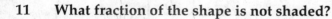

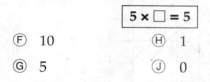

12 Which picture shows $\frac{2}{3}$ of the flowers shaded?

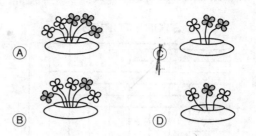

13 The pizza restaurant cuts each pizza into 6 slices. What is the missing number that completes the pattern in the chart?

Pizzas	Number of Slices
1	6
2	?
3	18
4	24

Ⓕ 1 Ⓗ 7

Ⓖ 6 Ⓙ 12

14 The students in Mrs. James' class must collect 20 leaves. The table shows the fraction of leaves each student has collected so far.

Name	Fraction Collected
Ken	$\frac{1}{4}$
Dominic	$\frac{1}{5}$
Jenna	$\frac{1}{10}$
Perry	$\frac{1}{2}$

Which student collected the smallest fraction of leaves?

Ⓐ Ken Ⓒ Jenna

Ⓑ Dominic Ⓓ Perry

The graph below shows the kinds of sports stories students in Ms. Kent's class wrote. Study the graph and answer questions 15 and 16.

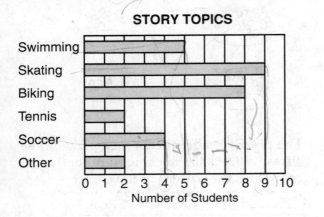

STORY TOPICS

15 How many students wrote about skating?

_____

_____

16 How many more students wrote about skating than soccer?

Ⓕ 5 Ⓗ 9

Ⓖ 7 Ⓙ 13

17 The tally chart shows the number of butterflies 4 students spotted during a week.

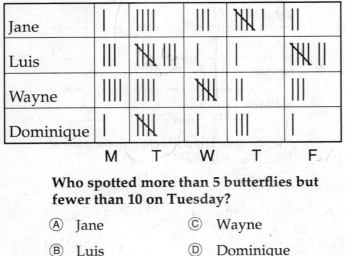

Who spotted more than 5 butterflies but fewer than 10 on Tuesday?

Ⓐ Jane Ⓒ Wayne

Ⓑ Luis Ⓓ Dominique

18 The chart below shows the number of ounces in cartons of juice.

Juice	Ounces
Orange	5.3
Apple	5.6
Grape	6.1
Cranberry	4.5

Which juice carton has the most ounces?

Ⓕ Orange Ⓗ Grape

Ⓖ Apple Ⓙ Cranberry

19 What is the missing number that completes the pattern in the boxes?

3	9	15	21	

Ⓐ 23 Ⓒ 27

Ⓑ 25 Ⓓ 30

20 Which shows the piece missing from the figure?

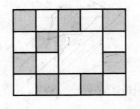

Ⓕ

Ⓗ

Ⓖ

Ⓙ

GO ON

110

21 Which names the location of 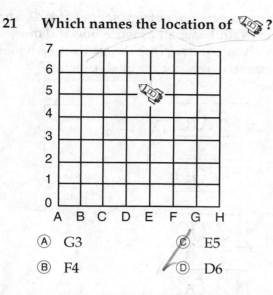?

Ⓐ G3 Ⓒ E5
Ⓑ F4 Ⓓ D6

22 Florence is playing a game with the spinner. Which month will the next spin least likely show?

December

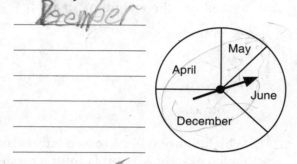

23 The table below shows the number of books students in Mrs. Wallin's class have read.

Name	Number of Books
Marilyn	18
Penny	27
Lillian	15
Kyle	30
Jim	29

Who read 14 more books than Lillian?

Ⓕ Jim Ⓗ Penny
Ⓖ Kyle Ⓙ Marilyn

24 Look at the numbered shapes. Which two figures are exactly the same in size and shape?

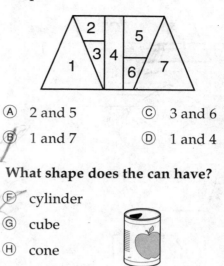

Ⓐ 2 and 5 Ⓒ 3 and 6
Ⓑ 1 and 7 Ⓓ 1 and 4

25 What shape does the can have?

Ⓕ cylinder
Ⓖ cube
Ⓗ cone
Ⓙ sphere

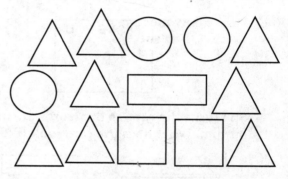

26 These shapes were picked from a bag.

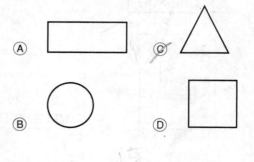

If one more shape is picked from the bag, which of these shapes will it most likely be?

Ⓐ ▭ Ⓒ △
Ⓑ ◯ Ⓓ ▢

GO ON

27 Which shape has four corners and four sides that are exactly the same length?

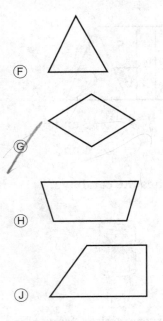

Ⓕ

Ⓖ

Ⓗ

Ⓙ

28 Clara made a card for her mother.

She turns the card so the words are on the bottom. What does the card look like now?

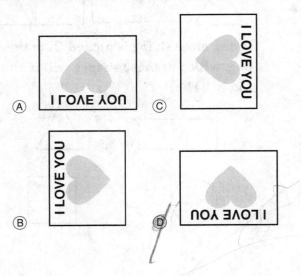

29 Carmen gets home from school at 3:30. She leaves for baseball practice one and one-half hours later. What time will it be when Carmen leaves for baseball practice?

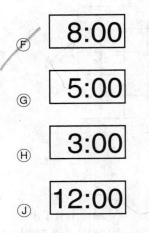

Ⓕ 8:00

Ⓖ 5:00

Ⓗ 3:00

Ⓙ 12:00

30 Which unit of measurement is best to use to measure the weight of an apple?

Ⓐ pounds

Ⓑ inches

Ⓒ quarts

Ⓓ ounces

31 Which figure will have two halves that match exactly when it is folded on the solid line?

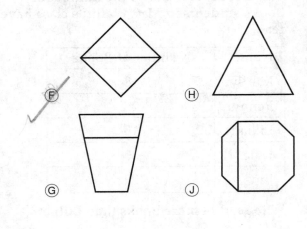

Ⓕ

Ⓖ

Ⓗ

Ⓙ

GO ON ▶

32 Carmine bought a football helmet that cost $9.84. He gave the store clerk $10.00. Which coins should Carmine receive in change?

Ⓐ

Ⓑ

Ⓒ

Ⓓ

33 Aris found these coins in his yard. What is the value of the money shown?

Ⓕ 36¢ Ⓗ 50¢

Ⓖ 41¢ Ⓙ 61¢

34 What temperature is shown on the thermometer?

Ⓐ 41°

Ⓑ 48°

Ⓒ 52°

Ⓓ 90°

50 ——— F

40 ———

35 How many inches long is the trail from where the squirrel is to the nuts? Use your inch ruler to answer this question.

Ⓕ 3 inches Ⓗ 7 inches

Ⓖ 5 inches Ⓙ 9 inches

36 A bird is building a nest. The lines show how far it flies to get the grass and twigs for the nest. Which line shows the longest distance the bird flies from the nest?

Ⓐ 1

Ⓑ 2

Ⓒ 3

Ⓓ 4

Nest

1 2 3 4

37 How many small squares in all are needed to fill the rectangle?

Ⓕ 25

Ⓖ 20

Ⓗ 15

Ⓙ 3

GO ON

38 Crystal is 5 years younger than Carlos. Carlos is 3 years younger than Don. Don is 13. How old is Crystal?

(A) 16　　(C) 5

(B) 10　　(D) 1

39 The table shows how the third-grade students at Main Street Elementary travel to school.

Way of Travel	Number of Students
Car	38
Bus	73
Bicycle	9
Walk	9

<u>About</u> how many third-grade students are there altogether?

(F) 80　　(H) 130

(G) 100　　(J) 140

40 <u>About</u> how much did Chip spend on 2 shirts and a jacket?

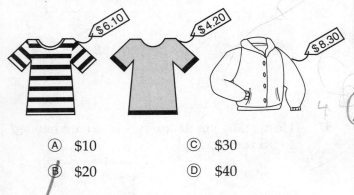

$6.10　$4.20　$8.30

(A) $10　　(C) $30

(B) $20　　(D) $40

41 What number is inside the circle, is outside the square, and is an even number?

(F) 11

(G) 12

(H) 13

(J) 15

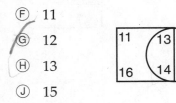

11　13　12
16　14　15

42 Mr. Takata put the top of his car down before going for a drive. What is the temperature outside like?

(A) 87°

(B) 41°

(C) 32°

(D) 15°

43 Dawn sold 15 calendars on Thursday. She sold 30 on Sunday. Which number sentence shows how to find the total number of calendars Dawn sold?

(F) 30 + 15 = □

(G) 30 − 15 = □

(H) □ + 15 = 30

(J) 30 × 15 = □

STOP

114

Part 2: Math Procedures

Sample A

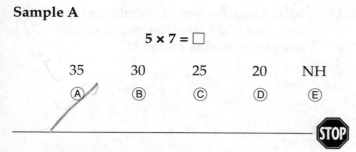

$$5 \times 7 = \square$$

35	30	25	20	NH
Ⓐ	Ⓑ	Ⓒ	Ⓓ	Ⓔ

🛑 **STOP**

For questions 1–22, darken the circle for the correct answer. If the correct answer is *Not Here*, darken the circle for *NH*. If no choices are given, write in the answer.

1

$$711$$
$$28$$
$$+\ 84$$

713	722	823	1831	NH
Ⓐ	Ⓑ	Ⓒ	Ⓓ	Ⓔ

2

$$324$$
$$-\ 228$$

94	97	104	106	NH
Ⓕ	Ⓖ	Ⓗ	Ⓙ	Ⓚ

3

$$7 + \square = 14$$

9	8	7	6	NH
Ⓐ	Ⓑ	Ⓒ	Ⓓ	Ⓔ

4

$$8$$
$$\times\ 8$$

16	56	64	72	NH
Ⓕ	Ⓖ	Ⓗ	Ⓙ	Ⓚ

5

$$95$$
$$-\ 16$$

111	101	89	79	NH
Ⓐ	Ⓑ	Ⓒ	Ⓓ	Ⓔ

6

$$625$$
$$+\ 39$$

654	664	754	764	NH
Ⓕ	Ⓖ	Ⓗ	Ⓙ	Ⓚ

7

$$648$$
$$-\ 63$$

8

$$46$$
$$+\ 27$$

You have 25 minutes to complete this test.

➤ GO ON

9

$$57 \times 9$$

4,563	453	456	156	NH
Ⓐ	Ⓑ	Ⓒ	Ⓓ	Ⓔ

10

$$50 \times 2 = \square$$

10	52	70	100	NH
Ⓕ	Ⓖ	Ⓗ	Ⓙ	Ⓚ

11

$$10 \times 64$$

74	110	604	640	NH
Ⓐ	Ⓑ	Ⓒ	Ⓓ	Ⓔ

12

$$123 \times 4$$

462	472	492	592	NH
Ⓕ	Ⓖ	Ⓗ	Ⓙ	Ⓚ

13

$$5 \overline{)35}$$

5	6	7	8	NH
Ⓐ	Ⓑ	Ⓒ	Ⓓ	Ⓔ

14

$$36 \div 6 = \square$$

---

15 Sally bought a bunch of balloons for $3.59. She paid $0.27 tax. How much did she pay altogether for the balloons?

$3.36	$3.72	$3.76	$3.82	NH
Ⓕ	Ⓖ	Ⓗ	Ⓙ	Ⓚ

---

16 Harbor Hills Elementary School has 789 students. What is that number rounded to the nearest hundred?

789

700	750	790	800	NH
Ⓐ	Ⓑ	Ⓒ	Ⓓ	Ⓔ

---

17 Amy saw 62 cars in one train. What is that number rounded to the nearest ten?

50	60	65	70	NH
Ⓕ	Ⓖ	Ⓗ	Ⓙ	Ⓚ

GO ON

Sample B

Roberto bought 11 pencils. Each pencil cost 7¢. How much did Roberto pay for all the pencils?

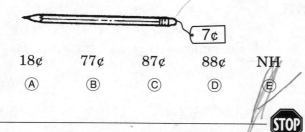

18¢	77¢	87¢	88¢	NH
Ⓐ	Ⓑ	Ⓒ	Ⓓ	Ⓔ

STOP

18 It takes the juice from 3 oranges to make a full glass of orange juice. Ed wants to make 5 glasses of juice. How many oranges does Ed need?

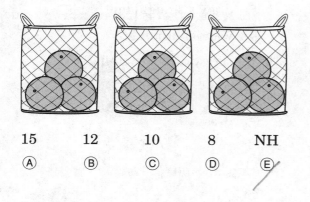

15	12	10	8	NH
Ⓐ	Ⓑ	Ⓒ	Ⓓ	Ⓔ

19 Fay made a list of all the toy animals she owns.

Mice	Bears	Dogs
15	3	9

How many toy animals does Fay own altogether?

12	18	24	27	NH
Ⓕ	Ⓖ	Ⓗ	Ⓙ	Ⓚ

20 Noriko cut 46 fabric squares for a quilt. There were 18 striped squares. The rest were solid colors. How many solid-colored squares did Noriko cut?

Ⓐ 28

Ⓑ 38

Ⓒ 63

Ⓓ 64

Ⓔ NH

21 Fran wants to buy this purse, which costs $10.00. She has $2.50. How much more money does she need to buy the purse?

$10.00

$7.50	$7.75	$8.25	$8.50	NH
Ⓕ	Ⓖ	Ⓗ	Ⓙ	Ⓚ

22 A group of 561 adults and 804 children went to the circus. How many more children than adults went on the outing?

343	333	243	233	NH
Ⓐ	Ⓑ	Ⓒ	Ⓓ	Ⓔ

STOP

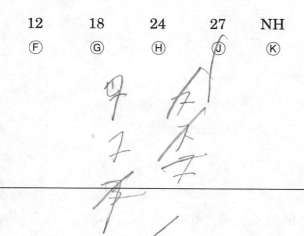

117

Listening

Sample A

- Ⓐ depressing
- Ⓑ encouraging
- Ⓒ frightening
- Ⓓ upsetting

STOP

For questions 1–12, darken the circle for the word or words that best complete the sentence you hear.

1
- Ⓐ tiny
- Ⓒ huge
- Ⓑ main
- Ⓓ important

2
- Ⓕ teenager
- Ⓖ student
- Ⓗ boss
- Ⓙ worker

3
- Ⓐ excite
- Ⓑ create
- Ⓒ ruin
- Ⓓ scatter

4
- Ⓕ trick them
- Ⓖ help them
- Ⓗ teach them
- Ⓙ harm them

5
- Ⓐ admire
- Ⓑ achieve
- Ⓒ rest
- Ⓓ discuss

6
- Ⓕ common
- Ⓗ pretend
- Ⓖ surprising
- Ⓙ grand

7
- Ⓐ birthday
- Ⓑ holiday
- Ⓒ weekday
- Ⓓ school day

8
- Ⓕ draw a straight line
- Ⓖ wander around
- Ⓗ slide down something
- Ⓙ run very fast

9
- Ⓐ dress
- Ⓑ coat
- Ⓒ snowsuit
- Ⓓ hat

10
- Ⓕ bargain
- Ⓖ settlement
- Ⓗ disagreement
- Ⓙ discussion

11
- Ⓐ solid
- Ⓑ narrow
- Ⓒ empty
- Ⓓ overflowing

12
- Ⓕ freedom
- Ⓖ slavery
- Ⓗ responsibility
- Ⓙ duty

STOP

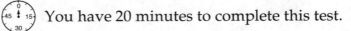 You have 20 minutes to complete this test.

Sample B

- Ⓐ hammer
- Ⓑ flashlight
- Ⓒ sandwich
- Ⓓ radio

STOP

For questions 13–24, listen to the story. Then darken the circle for the word or words that best answer the question.

13
- Ⓐ "Sleeping and Playing"
- Ⓑ "Kenji and His Playpen"
- Ⓒ "A Visit from Japan"
- Ⓓ "An Older Brother's Problem"

14
- Ⓕ loud
- Ⓖ tiny
- Ⓗ cute
- Ⓙ smart

15
- Ⓐ became tired
- Ⓑ liked the turtle
- Ⓒ stumbled and fell
- Ⓓ ran off to play

16
- Ⓕ never
- Ⓖ in the mornings
- Ⓗ in the evenings
- Ⓙ in the afternoons

17
- Ⓐ football
- Ⓑ basketball
- Ⓒ tennis
- Ⓓ baseball

18
- Ⓕ California
- Ⓖ Hawaii
- Ⓗ Chicago
- Ⓙ Texas

19
- Ⓐ sail on a boat
- Ⓑ ride in a car
- Ⓒ fly in a plane
- Ⓓ take a helicopter ride

20
- Ⓕ grandparents
- Ⓖ parents
- Ⓗ best friends
- Ⓙ aunt and uncle

21
- Ⓐ shopping
- Ⓑ on a sleigh ride
- Ⓒ ice-skating
- Ⓓ to roast marshmallows

22
- Ⓕ angry
- Ⓖ scared
- Ⓗ proud
- Ⓙ worried

23
- Ⓐ a flag
- Ⓑ a window
- Ⓒ the door
- Ⓓ another tower

24
- Ⓕ floor
- Ⓖ lawn
- Ⓗ beach
- Ⓙ sidewalk

STOP

Language

Sample A

Let's Get a Pet

Kelly wants to have a pet. She's not sure what kind of pet she wants. Kelly's cousin Maureen has a few pets. Kelly decides to write Maureen a letter to find out which pet she likes best.

Why is Kelly writing this letter?

Ⓐ to find out more about kittens

Ⓑ to help her decide what pet to get

Ⓒ to help her parents learn more about pets

Ⓓ to learn to write better letters

For questions 1–4, darken the circle for the correct answer, or write in the answer.

Kelly found the book *Taking Care of a Pet* in the library. Use part of the Index from this book to answer questions 1 and 2.

Index

aquarium pets
    first aid and diseases, 248–249
beds
    for cats, 33
    for dogs, 21–22
cages
    canaries, 62–63
    hamsters, 54–55
    white mice, 51
first aid, 231–254
rabbits
    cleanliness, 42, 44
    handling, 41–42
    teeth, 44–45

1 **Information about first aid for pets can be found on all these pages <u>except</u>—**

    232   245   250   260
    Ⓐ   Ⓑ   Ⓒ   Ⓓ

2 **Kelly can find information about cages for white mice on which pages?**

_____

3 **Kelly put these words in alphabetical (*ABC*) order so she could find them more quickly in the dictionary. Which list is correct?**

Ⓕ guinea pigs – gerbils – goldfish – guppies

Ⓖ guppies – guinea pigs – goldfish – gerbils

Ⓗ guppies – gerbils – goldfish – guinea pigs

Ⓙ gerbils – goldfish – guinea pigs – guppies

4 **Kelly found the book *How to Take Care of a Pet*. Where should she look to find the author's name?**

Ⓐ Chapter 1

Ⓑ the title page

Ⓒ the index

Ⓓ the table of contents

GO ON

You have 30 minutes to complete this test.

Here is the first part of Kelly's letter. Read it carefully. Then answer questions 5–8.

> Dear Maureen,
>
> How are you doing? Are your pets doing well? I can get a
> (1)   (2)   (3)
>
> pet my mom and dad told me. Now I need to decide. Which
>   (4)   (5)
>
> one to get. My mom and dad bought me a new bicycle. I think
>   (6)   (7)
>
> having a pet will be fun. I know it's a big responsibility. Mom
>   (8)   (9)
>
> told me that I would have to take care of it. I'll have to give it
>   (10)
>
> food and water. I'll have to make it comfortable. I can't wait to
>   (11)   (12)
>
> do all this. That's why I'm writing to you.
>   (13)

5 **The best way to write sentence 3 is—**

Ⓕ My mom and dad told me that I can get a pet.

Ⓖ My mom told me that I can get a pet, my dad, too.

Ⓗ A pet my mom and dad told me I can get.

Ⓙ As it is written.

6 **Which group of words is not a complete sentence? Write the number of the group of words.**

_____

_____

_____

_____

7 **Which of these sentences could be added after sentence 13?**

Ⓐ Kittens are fun to have as pets.

Ⓑ Do you have a new bicycle?

Ⓒ What pet do you think I should get?

Ⓓ Will you be able to come to my house?

8 **Which sentence does not belong in Kelly's letter?**

6	7	8	10
Ⓕ	Ⓖ	Ⓗ	Ⓙ

121

Here is the next part of Kelly's letter. This part has groups of words underlined. Read the letter carefully. Then answer questions 9–14.

There are many pets I'd like to get. I would love to have <u>a kitten</u>
(14)   (15)
<u>a puppy, and a hamster.</u> Dad says I have to choose one. A kitten
(16)   (17)
<u>might be a good pet</u> for me. Kittens love to be cuddled. I would
(18)   (19)
be very gentle with it when I held it. <u>Kittens is very</u> playful. They
(20)   (21)
love to play with little balls and string. Kittens <u>needed to be fed</u>
(22)
every day. <u>Do you think an kitten</u> would be a good pet for me?
(23)

sincerely yours,
Kelly

9 In sentence 15, <u>a kitten a puppy, and a hamster.</u> is best written—

Ⓐ a kitten a puppy and a hamster.

Ⓑ a kitten, a puppy and a hamster.

Ⓒ a kitten, a puppy, and a hamster.

Ⓓ As it is written.

10 In sentence 17, <u>might be a good pet</u> is best written—

Ⓕ a good pet might be

Ⓖ might a good pet be

Ⓗ be a might good pet

Ⓙ As it is written.

11 In sentence 20, <u>Kittens is very</u> is best written—

Ⓐ Kittens are very

Ⓑ Kittens were very

Ⓒ Kittens am very

Ⓓ As it is written.

▶GO ON

12 In sentence 22, <u>needed to be fed</u> is best written—

   Ⓕ needs to be fed

   Ⓖ need to be fed

   Ⓗ needing to be fed

   Ⓙ As it is written.

13 In sentence 23, <u>Do you think an kitten</u> is best written—

   Ⓐ Do you thinks an kitten

   Ⓑ Do you thinks a kitten

   Ⓒ Do you think a kitten

   Ⓓ As it is written.

14 At the end of Kelly's letter, <u>sincerely yours,</u> is best written—

   Ⓕ Sincerely Yours,

   Ⓖ Sincerely yours,

   Ⓗ sincerely Yours,

   Ⓙ As it is written.

▶GO ON▶

Drew is writing a report on his trip to Arizona. Read the following. Then answer questions 15–18.

> ## A Dry Land
>
> Drew's teacher wants the class to write a report about their favorite vacation. Drew enjoyed seeing the desert. So, Drew decided to write his report about his trip to Arizona.

15 **What is the first thing Drew should do before he begins to write his paper?**

(A) Remember what other vacations were like.

(B) Buy books about deserts.

(C) Make a list of what he saw in the desert.

(D) Ask his sister to write about the desert, too.

16 **If Drew wants to find the meaning of the word cactus, where should he look first?**

(F) an encyclopedia

(G) a dictionary

(H) a language arts book

(J) an atlas

17 **If Drew wants to learn more about deserts, he should look in—**

(A) an encyclopedia.

(B) a dictionary.

(C) a newspaper.

(D) a language arts book.

Before Drew begins his report, he looks up some words in the dictionary.

18 **What definintion best fits the word dry as used in the sentence below? Write the definition.**

Some plants grow well in a *dry* climate.

_____

_____

_____

_____

_____

_____

_____

GO ON

Here is the first part of Drew's report. Read it carefully. Then answer questions 19–23.

Sunny Arizona

We stayed in hotels. We visited during the day many places.
   (1)   (2)

We had to drive many miles. Last year we visited Maine. Most
(3)   (4)   (5)

of the time we drove through a desert. I couldn't believe how
                                  (6)

big it was. It is very dry in a desert. It is very sunny in a
        (7)   (8)

desert. A place is called a desert. If it gets less than ten inches
   (9)   (10)

of rain each year. Staying in a desert makes you thirsty. We
      (11)   (12)

made sure that we had plenty of water to drink.

---

19 **Which sentence would best begin this paragraph?**

Ⓕ I like to go on vacation.

Ⓖ My vacation to Arizona was so much fun!

Ⓗ Next year we plan to visit Texas.

Ⓙ Summer vacation starts in two weeks.

20 **The best way to write sentence 2 is—**

Ⓐ During the day many places we visited.

Ⓑ During the day we visited many places.

Ⓒ Many places we visited during the day.

Ⓓ As it is written.

▶**GO ON**

21 Which sentence does <u>not</u> belong in Drew's report? Write the number of the sentence.

_____

_____ Last ____ ____

_____

_____

22 Which of these is <u>not</u> a complete sentence?

    5   7   10   12
   Ⓕ   Ⓖ   Ⓗ   Ⓙ

23 What is the best way to combine sentences 7 and 8 without changing their meaning?

Ⓐ Since it is very sunny it is dry in a desert.

Ⓑ It is very dry in a desert and it is very sunny.

Ⓒ Being very dry it is also very sunny in a desert.

Ⓓ It is very dry and sunny in a desert.

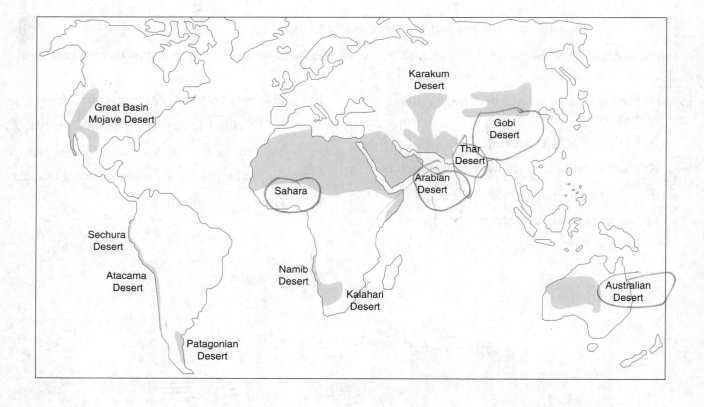

GO ON

Here is the next part of Drew's report. This part has groups of words underlined. Read the draft carefully. Then answer questions 24–27.

I used to think <u>that an desert</u> was just all sand. Some deserts
(13)   (14)
in the world are mostly sand. The desert that I saw in Arizona
(15)
has some interesting plants. One plant I saw was the cactus. This
(16)   (17)
kind of plant can survive with very little rain. <u>I also seen</u> clumps
(18)
of grass. At certain times of the year <u>a Desert does get</u> some
(19)
rain. That's when you can see many colorful flowering plants. I
(20)   (21)
think the desert was a very interesting place to visit. I hope <u>I can</u>
(22)
<u>visit it again</u> someday.

24 In sentence 13, <u>that an desert</u> is best written—

Ⓕ that a deserts

Ⓖ that an deserts

Ⓗ that a desert

Ⓙ As it is written.

25 In sentence 18, <u>I also seen</u> is best written—

Ⓐ I also saw

Ⓑ I also see

Ⓒ I also sees

Ⓓ As it is written.

26 In sentence 19, <u>a Desert does get</u> is best written—

Ⓕ a desert do get

Ⓖ a desert does get

Ⓗ a Desert do get

Ⓙ As it is written.

27 In sentence 22, <u>I can visit it again</u> is best written—

Ⓐ I cans visit it again

Ⓑ i can visit it again

Ⓒ I, can visit it again

Ⓓ As it is written.

▶GO ON▶

For questions 28–35, read each sentence carefully. If one of the words is misspelled, darken the circle for that word. If all the words are spelled correctly, then darken the circle for *No mistake*.

28   The children <u>laughd</u> at the <u>circus</u> <u>clowns</u>. <u>No mistake</u>
                F   G   H   J

29   We <u>watched</u> the snow <u>falling</u> on the <u>mowntan</u>. <u>No mistake</u>
         A   B   C   D

30   We <u>collected</u> <u>colorful</u> seashells on the <u>beachs</u> of Hawaii. <u>No mistake</u>
        F   G   H   J

31   This <u>apple</u> is <u>sweet</u> and <u>juicy</u>! <u>No mistake</u>
        A   B   C   D

32   The <u>family</u> was able to <u>safly</u> leave the <u>burning</u> house. <u>No mistake</u>
        F   G   H   J

33   The <u>tinyest</u> <u>kitten</u> is black and <u>white</u>. <u>No mistake</u>
        A   B   C   D

34   Birds built nests in the <u>branchs</u> of the <u>oak</u> <u>trees</u>. <u>No mistake</u>
                     F   G   H   J

35   Lynn threw a <u>penny</u> into the <u>wishing</u> <u>well</u>. <u>No mistake</u>
           A   B   C   D

STOP

Individual Record Form

This table lists all the tests in *Core Skills: Test Preparation, Grade 3.* It also lists the number of questions in each test and the page on which the test is located. Use the table to track your child's performance by recording the number of correct answers he or she gives on each test. Use the back of the page to record notes about your child's strengths, weaknesses, and progress.

Test Area and Skill	Pages	Number of Questions	Number Right
Reading Comprehension			
Reading Selections	33–40	30	
Test	41–47	28	
Reading Vocabulary			
Understanding Word Meanings	48	6	
Matching Words with More Than One Meaning	49	4	
Using Context Clues	50	6	
Test	51–53	21	
Math Problem Solving and Procedures			
Understanding Numeration	57	4	
Using Whole Numbers, Fractions, and Decimals	58	5	
Understanding Patterns and Relationships	59	4	
Working with Statistics and Probability	60	7	
Understanding Geometry	62	4	
Working with Measurement	63	7	
Solving Problems	65	4	
Understanding Computation	66	8	
Using Computation	67	4	
Test 1: Math Procedures	68–69	14	
Test 2: Math Problem Solving	70–77	44	
Listening			
Listening for Word Meanings	78	8	
Building Listening Skills	79	8	
Test	80–81	23	
Language			
Prewriting, Composing, and Editing	82–88	25	
Identifying Misspelled Words	89	5	
Test	90–96	32	
Practice Test 1			
Reading Comprehension	97–104	32	
Practice Test 2			
Reading Vocabulary	105–107	21	
Practice Test 3			
Part 1: Math Problem Solving	108–114	43	
Part 2: Math Procedures	115–117	22	
Practice Test 4			
Listening	118–119	22	
Practice Test 5			
Language	120–128	35	